LIVING ETHICALLY IN THE '90s

LIVING ETHICALLY IN THE '90s

J. KERBY ANDERSON, EDITOR

VICTOR BOOKS®

A DIVISION OF SCRIPTURE PRESS PUBLICATIONS INC.
USA CANADA ENGLAND

Scripture quotations unless otherwise indicated are from the *Holy Bible, New International Version*, © 1973, 1978, 1984, International Bible Society. Used by permission of Zondervan Bible Publishers.

Library of Congress Cataloging-in-Publication Data

Anderson, J. Kerby.
    Living ethically in the '90s / by J. Kerby Anderson.
       p.   cm.
    Includes bibliographical references.
    ISBN 0-89693-012-2
    1. Christian ethics. 2. Church and social problems—United States.
3. Evangelicalism. 4. United States—Moral conditions. 5. Fundamentalism.   I. Title. II. Title: Living ethically in the nineties.
BJ1251.A47   1990
241—dc20   89-49773
                                               CIP

VICTOR BOOKS
A division of Scripture Press
Wheaton, Illinois 60187

CONTENTS

FOREWORD

God's clearly stated job description for man was to govern His world, to develop and regulate the earth for God's glory and man's benefit. Gigantic human error nearly neutralized the plan, but after the Flood the Creator graciously gave a second chance. Still man continued to emphasize his own personal welfare over the exaltation of the Almighty. He preferred to blend with rather than separate from evil.

Christians are called to make a difference by being different. We are not to be *of* the world but we are most certainly *in* a complex and pressurized community. Faith is validated in the loneliness of personal compliance with God's commands. The Prophet Micah boiled it all down to one question: "What does the Lord require of you?" Answer: "To act justly and to love mercy and to walk humbly with your God."

Our latter-day report card reflects no improvement in the subjects of justice, mercy, and humility. We evangelicals have often been remiss in tackling these tough topics. Fashionable pulpits tend less and less to bother with theology. Issues of God's glory are occluded, His Word downgraded.

Through *Bibliotheca Sacra* Dallas Seminary has sought to contribute to matters of moral living. Now in this one collection, themes touching legal, medical, and social ethics are brought together. We who desire to be in the forefront of biblical thinking must address solutions beyond superficial furnishings. Our private ideas are dangerously limited unless we reap the fertile fields of other minds. We cannot love mercy when we refuse to deal realistically with all aspects of heartlessness. Nor can we walk humbly with our God if we disregard the processes of pride. Justice is the child of sound doctrine. This volume is a generator, to propel the reader forward along the path to leadership of informed integrity.

Howard G. Hendricks
Center for Christian Leadership
Dallas Theological Seminary

■ ■ ■ ■ ■ ■ ■ ■ ■

MORAL
AND
SOCIAL
ISSUES

1
CRISIS IN MORALITY
Erwin W. Lutzer

S ituation ethics is everywhere in this generation: *"That's just your belief." "It's your decision." "It may be wrong for you, but not for me."* It is making decisions believing that there are no universal moral principles, that only the situation determines what is moral or immoral. Its summary rule is: *Do the most loving thing.*

Joseph Fletcher is the principal spokesman for "situationism." He delineates three of its major facets:
1. A loving act is one done with loving intentions.
2. The end justifies the means.
3. An act can be judged as loving or unloving because of the consequences.

Can situationism survive analysis? If it can, it is a serious alternative to biblical ethics.

However, there are difficulties that advocates of situation ethics must face. Only when these problems are solved can the theory be taken as an alternative to biblical morality.

THE IMPOSSIBILITY OF LOVE DEFINING THE CONTENT OF MORAL OBLIGATION

Fletcher's situation ethics system is built on the premise that love is the only absolute in ethical conduct. What is loving is determined not by a universal rule, but by the situation.

However, even if one knows all the facts, love cannot of itself give guidance in making ethical choices. Behind every moral decision lies the decision of what should be regarded as valuable and by what scale values should be judged. We all make decisions from day to day on the basis of our own value systems. Some may consider money of greater value than education. Some prefer prestige to sexual purity. Some consider Communism of more value than Christianity. Others prefer drunkenness to sobriety. All these decisions are made on the basis of personal values.

Hitler achieved what he believed were worthy ends according to his personal values. Others have done the same, and the situationists agree with some of them. Fletcher says that "a Viet Cong terrorist walking into a Saigon officers' mess as he pulls the pin in a bomb hidden under his coat" is an example of an altruistic ethic.[1] Similar illustrations "are examples of selfless, calculating concern for others."[2] And Fletcher is right—given the Viet Cong's system of values.

Another incident Fletcher discusses occurred during World War II when a priest bombed a Nazi freight train. In response, the Nazis killed 20 hostages a day until the guilty person surrendered. Three days later a Communist (a fellow resistance fighter) betrayed the priest. When asked why he refused to give himself up, the priest said, "There is no other priest available, and our people's souls need my absolution for their eternal salvation."[3]

This incident is recorded two-thirds of the way through Fletcher's book *Situation Ethics*. Having read this far, one would expect Fletcher to say that the priest was not doing the most loving thing. But Fletcher (startling though it may be) says, "One may accept the priest's assumptions about salvation or not (the Communist evidently did not), but no situationist could quarrel with his method of ethical analysis and decision."[4] Given the priest's set of values, he was doing the most loving thing. But the Communist also thought he was doing the most loving thing in stopping the daily massacre.

Because they could not agree on a system of values, they could not agree on an ethical decision.

This illustration shows with horrifying clarity the problem of situationism. How can values be weighed?

Fletcher might also have given illustrations of biblical characters whose actions were motivated by their value systems. They believed that present sufferings are not worth comparing with the glory that will be revealed in us (Rom. 8:18). Fletcher might have said, "One may or may not accept their view of eternity, but no situationist can quarrel with their method of ethical analysis and decision."

In this sense, Fletcher could say that Christ also was a sitationist when He went to the cross. Clearly, His value system differed radically from Fletcher's, and He did not follow Fletcher's suggestions on how to be a hypocrite to avoid undesirable earthly consequences by only pretending He had devotion to God the Father.[5] But Christ's actions were loving: "The Son of man did not come to be served but to serve, and to give His life as a ransom for many" (Mark 10:45). He calculated the eternal consequences of fulfilling the commandments of God the Father.

Moses believed that the most loving thing was to turn from earthly riches and to follow God. On the other hand, Lenin believed that a classless society was of more value than the lives of the people massacred to bring it about. The leaders of the Inquisition believed that the eternal salvation of a few was of more value than the physical lives of the heretics. The Hindu lady throws the best of her two babies into the Ganges River because she believes the gods will reward her and her family by providing food and keeping evil spirits away. A criminal, Communist, Catholic, Puritan, Christian, Protestant, and Hindu can all be situationists; that is, they are all doing the most loving thing in harmony with their system of values. However, the crucial question is: Whose values are right?

Fletcher cannot escape the fact that he has provided no solutions as to what ends are to be sought. Apart from his private moral judgments, no attempt is made to provide coherent reasons for his value judgments. His summary rule of love is equivalent to a football game where only one summary rule exists: fair play. Any other rule he classifies as "legalism." A game of football played with Fletcher's "rule" of fair play, where no referee is allowed to interfere and each player does what is right in his own eyes, would be full of confusion. Fair play does not provide rules for playing a game; similarly, love does not give direction for making moral choices.

THE IMPOSSIBILITY OF PREDICTING CONSEQUENCES

Suppose that all of the theological and philosophical debates of the past were finally settled, and situationism *would* be able to give a detailed account of which ends are valuable. It still could not give moral direction, because it is impossible to predict accurately the consequences of one's actions. In other words, one could never be sure if the means employed would achieve the desired ends. Situationism's axiom that one can judge whether an act is loving or unloving by its consequences, and that therefore the end justifies the means, is impossible to carry out.

Even Fletcher candidly admits, "We can't always guess the future, even though we are always being forced to try."[6] Yet the fact is that unless certain desired consequences result, the action is then immoral in their eyes.

Fletcher attempts to avoid this criticism of situationism by simply ignoring it. In places he modestly admits that there is human error and that situationism "presumes more ability to know the facts and weigh them than most people can muster."[7] But for the most part he assumes that consequences can be easily predicted and tabulated.

Situationism is untenable in practice, however. If an action is right when it helps someone, then a lie could be moral until it is discovered. Afterward it can result in greater harm for the greatest number. If Fletcher were to say that a lie is moral because of good intentions, he would be contradicting his basic thesis that only what helps people is good. Also, he would be falling into the very error he elsewhere deplores, because to assert that a lie is moral merely because of good motives (apart from good consequences) is to have what is called an intrinsic view of right and wrong: that the lie is inherently right regardless of the outcome. If this is what Fletcher believes, he cannot criticize those who insist that a lie is always evil apart from its outcome!

In conclusion, if the situationists are correct, the probability of knowing beforehand the results of one's actions is so remote that no individual could make an ethical judgment with certainty. In fact, no decision could be classified as moral until all the results were tabulated and weighed mathematically. On a practical level, morality then would be impossible.

THE IMPOSSIBILITY OF HOLDING TO A RELATIVE ETHIC

Situationist philosophers believe that love is the highest good. However, at the same time they believe there is no ultimate or intrinsic good. Fletcher states, "The good is what works, what is expedient, what gives satisfaction."[8] Therefore, may not the day come when love will not work anymore?

Fletcher acknowledges this problem: "But it is of special importance here to emphasize from the situationist's angle of vision, that ends, like means, are relative, that all ends and means are related to each other in a contributory hierarchy, and that in their turn all ends become means to some end higher than themselves."[9]

This is a summary exposition of the pragmatic-relativistic philosophy that situationists embrace. Both ends and means are relative. What is good today may not be good tomorrow. In the very next sentence of the same paragraph, Fletcher resorts to his absolute. He says, "There is only one end, one goal, one purpose which is not relative and contingent, always an end in itself. Love."[10] But what shall be made of the previous statement that ends also are relative? And since all ends become means to higher ends, how can Fletcher be sure that love will always be the ultimate end? May not love be a means to another end which in turn is a means to another, ad infinitum? But if Fletcher's relativism is true, why might not love itself already be an obsolete end? In fact, the day might come when every value judgment made by Fletcher could be reversed. Moralists may begin to value principles more than people, hate may be substituted for love, and cannibalism might replace situationism. Could Fletcher give a reasoned argument against such a change? The answer must be no. As he wrote, both ends and means are relative. What is good today may be evil tomorrow.

Like a spider attempting to build a web on the moving hands of a clock, Fletcher attempts to establish a solid anchor with an ethical theory which by definition cannot have an unchangeable absolute. As has been stated, Fletcher may be granted his basic value, but when he combines this absolute with relativism, his system has a serious contradiction. Logically, if situationism (based on relativism) is true, then it is false (love no longer remains as the ultimate end).

CONCLUSION

Holding that law and love can never be harmonized, Joseph Fletcher as the spokesperson for situationism decided to make love superior to law. Therefore his ethical system cannot provide rules for moral conduct. If Fletcher argues (without constructing rules) that certain types of actions are unloving, three related factors must be considered. First, his standards as to why an action is generally unloving must be given. This involves the question of values, so he would have to give a detailed defense of what is a valuable loving end and what is not. Second, Fletcher would have to find a method to predict and calculate the consequences of action. Only in this way could one be certain of doing a moral act. Third, he would have to solve the problem that relativism cannot predict what will be loving in the future. Since the end justifies the means—and even the ends and means are relative—even love itself may no longer be a legitimate end. It follows that no conduct can therefore be judged as good or evil.

Fletcher says, "No 20th-century man of even average training will turn his back on the anthropological and psychological evidence for relativity in morals."[11] Recognizing the consequences of relativism, he later writes, "After all, it is not necessary to agree on an ethic to achieve living unity. . . ."[12] If these statements are true, 20th-century man will have to accept without rebuke legalism, rioting, cannibalism, genocide, massacre, and despair.

NOTES

1. Joseph Fletcher, *Situation Ethics* (Philadelphia: Westminster Press, 1966), 110.
2. Ibid.
3. Ibid., 115.
4. Ibid., 115–16.
5. Ibid., 72.
6. Ibid., 136.
7. Ibid., 84.
8. Ibid., 42.
9. Ibid., 129.
10. Ibid.
11. Ibid., 76.
12. Ibid., 159.

2
MORAL ENTROPY, CREATION, AND THE BATTLE FOR THE MIND
Kenneth O. Gangel

Everything is going downhill.

In science it's called the second law of thermodynamics. This states that disorder in a closed system increases with time. There is *entropy,* the dissolution of matter and energy in the universe to an ultimate state of inert uniformity.

This chapter proposes that there is also the problem of moral entropy, which may be dubbed "the law of theo-dynamics." This principle holds that the moral, spiritual, ethical, and cultural qualities of society are consistently deteriorating because of the presence of sin. It is stoppable only by the return of the Lord of Creation Himself.

Everything is going downhill. It's a terribly pessimistic subject without God, and even then the open-eyed realist in the late 20th century certainly must view the world around him with an awesome concern for its headlong plunge into Satan's stronghold.

DEMONSTRATION OF THE PROBLEM

Biblical Patterns

James Oliver Buswell, one of the great evangelical theologians of the 20th century, argues that we have to believe that the

sin of Adam really happened in order to understand this problem of sin in today's world. Neoorthodox and existential theol-
ogies with their mythical view of the early chapters of Genesis
may accept some doctrine of original sin, but they do not
believe that the Fall of man was a particular event which took
place in history.

However, the early chapters of Genesis can be trusted to
give a definitive account of the beginnings of the battle for the
mind. It is interesting that, as Francis Schaeffer points out,
"Absolutely every place where the New Testament refers to
the first half of Genesis, the New Testament assumes (and
many times affirms) that Genesis is history, and that it is to be
read in normal fashion with the common use of the words and
syntax."[1] In addition, all the New Testament writers except
James refer to Genesis 1:27, and all of their references are
positive in nature.[2] If we do not believe Scripture that the sin
of Adam was a representative act and that the Fall was a
historical event, the atonement itself can be questioned "as a
literally accomplished fact, a transaction once and for all, at the
cross of Calvary."[3]

If we assume the historicity of Adam's sin, the first six
chapters of the Book of Genesis offer a clear demonstration of
moral entropy in action, as the following texts affirm: "God
saw all that He had made, and it was very good" (Gen. 1:31)
.... "The man and his wife were both naked, and they felt no
shame" (2:25).... "To Adam he said, 'Because you listened
to your wife and ate from the tree about which I commanded
you, "You must not eat of it," cursed is the ground because of
you; through painful toil you will eat of it all the days of your
life. It will produce thorns and thistles for you, and you will eat
the plants of the field. By the sweat of your brow you will eat
your food until you return to the ground, since from it you
were taken; for dust you are and to dust you will return'"
(3:17-19).... "Now Cain said to his brother Abel, 'Let's go
out to the field.' And while they were in the field, Cain attacked his brother Abel and killed him" (4:8).... "Lamech
said to his wives, 'Adah and Zillah, listen to me; wives of

19

Lamech, hear my words. I have killed a man for wounding me, a young man for injuring me' " (4:23). . . . "The Lord saw how great man's wickedness on the earth had become, and that every inclination of the thoughts of his heart was only evil all the time. The Lord was grieved that he had made man on the earth, and his heart was filled with pain. So the Lord said, 'I will wipe mankind, whom I have created, from the face of the earth—men and animals, and creatures that move along the ground, and birds of the air—for I am grieved that I have made them' " (6:5-7).

The first text states that the original creation was good, and the second follows with the statement that immorality was unknown in the first family. Then the serpent acted, and the curse on Adam brought with it not only painful toil but also the prospect of physical death. Then Adam's son became a murderer, and later Lamech. This sad start to the first sinful civilization came to a culmination just before the Flood. The Fall affected the mind of man to such an extent that "every inclination of the thoughts of his heart was only evil all the time" (6:5).

It is clear that whatever the number of years between Adam and Noah, man's moral condition was all downward. No wonder Isaiah said about humanity that like sheep, we "have gone astray, each of us has turned to his own way" (Isa. 53:6).

But surely things improved in the New Testament times, some may argue. The very presence of God's Holy Son on the earth should have cleaned up the system, stemmed the tide of moral entropy, and turned the minds of people back to the Creator. Not so, Paul wrote. "The wrath of God is being revealed from heaven against all the godlessness and wickedness of men who suppress the truth by their wickedness, since what may be known about God is plain to them, because God has made it plain to them. For since the creation of the world God's invisible qualities—His eternal power and divine nature—have been clearly seen, being understood from what has been made, so that men are without excuse" (Rom. 1:18-20).

Natural Patterns

Things have not improved since Paul's day. Business and professional ethics have so deteriorated in society that even the secular press bemoans the low level of morality in contemporary Western culture. This demonstrates what Buswell calls "the sense of ought," a transcultural and timeless, innate grasp of right and wrong, derived from initial creation by God Himself.

> The fact that man generally has a moral sense, regardless of the inconsistencies in the outworking of this moral sense, seems to me to constitute evidence that man has fallen from a higher status. How could a mere naturalistic evolutionary process ever give rise to the sense of moral obligation, not mere desire, obligation to moral standards which ought to be realized regardless of desire?[4]

The blunting of the sense of ought or, as Paul puts it, the searing of one's conscience "as with a hot iron" (1 Tim. 4:2), is further complicated in the natural pattern of moral entropy by what might be called unrealized capacities. A race that has the capacity to design computers and split atoms and do even more has great responsibilities.

Also included in the natural pattern of moral entropy is the problem of disordered drives. Men like Hitler and Mao Tsetung possessed an undeniable genius, but the corruption of their brilliant minds by sin led to a utilization of creative powers toward evil rather than good.

Psychological Patterns

This "law of theo-dynamics" (moral entropy) is aptly observable in the psychological realm. Three behaviors are literally rampant on a worldwide scale in contemporary culture: inhumanity, abnormality, and irresponsibility.

Nations tremble with anarchy in the streets; political assassinations are systematically carried out in Third World countries; revolution and civil war can be found in multiple locations on various continents; and the concept of human rights has become a political football to justify or condemn whatever the user of the phrase wishes to defend or attack. Man's inhumanity to man is possibly the most obvious evidence that human minds are corrupted by sin. Zoologists point out that there is no observable cruelty among animals comparable to the cruelty which man sometimes exhibits toward his peers.

The matter of abnormality offers additional negative support for moral entropy. Barbour argued as early as 1930 that many of the facts of the disordered mind are better explained by the biblical view that they result from sin, than by such popular secular theories as the mythological "unconscious" or the "id" (Freud) or "racial memories" or the "collective unconscious" (Jung)[5] or, I would add, the popular Skinnerian excuse of blaming everything on one's environment.

Irresponsibility poses a third problem in the psychological arena. The Apostle Paul was appalled by the fact that the wicked world, knowing God's righteous decree, not only does things deserving of death, but regularly approves those who practice them (Rom. 1:32). There is no wonder Carl Henry referred to modern technological society as a "barbarian culture." Even the secular psychiatrist Menninger asked, "Whatever became of sin?"[6] The answer to Menninger's question is that many people have worked out a peaceful coexistence with sin.

The nature of capitalism in America requires individuals to be innovative, risk-taking, and competitive, while contemporary American education tends to foster dependency from the cradle to the grave. We take inhumanity, abnormality, and irresponsibility for granted while downgrading true humanity, normality, and responsibility as out-of-date values. Carl Henry quotes Malcom Muggeridge on this point: "The most extraordinary thing about human beings is the fact that they pursue ends which they know to be disastrous and turn their backs on ways which they know to be joyous."[7]

DESCRIPTION OF THE DILEMMA

Individually, Man's Mind Is Corrupt from Within

Jesus said, "Out of the overflow of the heart the mouth speaks. The good man brings good things out of the good stored up in him, and the evil man brings evil things out of the evil stored up in him" (Matt. 12:34-35). Sin continues because it finds a point of contact with the sinful self within. Thomas Howard urges Christians to let their minds be guided by "the touchstone of orthodoxy" and declares that there is no moral democracy any more than there is a mathematical democracy:

> A hundred years ago or a thousand or ten thousand, for that matter, mountebanks and wizards and false prophets had to whip up what following they could on the strength of their own voice and their own tricks. Now every jester has an instant, vast, and utterly credulous audience via the talk shows. The audience is credulous, I say, because they have been schooled in the tradition of moral and intellectual democracy, in which every idea is worth exactly as much as every other idea, and in which we are committed to giving equal time, not just on the air or in the columns of newsprint, but also in our minds—equal time, I say to Isaiah and Beelzebub, for example, or to St. Thomas Aquinas and Mick Jagger, or the blessed virgin and Bella Abzug. We see the talk show hosts, sitting in vapid amiability while their lively guests dismantle the entirety of history and myth, and we pick up this frame of mind. We take on an earnest, humorless frame of mind that gravely receives all data as "input," so that we hear one person telling us about the joys of open marriage, and another about what an emancipation it is to find that one is no longer a man or a woman but a person, and still another when we learn to address God as our androgyne which art in heaven—we hear all this, and our only response is, "What I hear you saying is. . ." or "I

23

need this input" or "Heavy," or some such trenchant comment.[8]

Yes, the battle for the mind rages on the individual level, but the words of Jesus still echo: "Love the Lord your God with all your heart, with all your soul and all your mind" (Matthew 22:37).

Socially, the Collectivity of Corrupt Minds Is Tearing the Universe Apart

It was the Apostle Paul, again, who warned of the disastrous social effect a united group of diseased minds could wreak on a culture: "The mind of sinful man is death . . . the sinful mind is hostile to God. It does not submit to God's law, nor can it do so. Those controlled by their sinful nature cannot please God" (Rom. 8:6-8).

One example of a mind which cannot please God because of its earthly orientation is the new humanism. Note how such philosophers as economist Kenneth Boulding are delighted with the progress of human society. Boulding says that modern man has lived through the dramatic crisis and now it is possible for man to begin developing his full potentials and capacities.[9] Soon man will be able to overcome poverty, disease, famine, and possibly even war. The coming of the knowledge explosion is irreversible, and Boulding is enthusiastic. One may think, rather, that Boulding has been born several decades too late. Such naive pronouncements of juvenile optimism marked the turn of the century, only to be buried by two world wars, a depression, and continuing cynicism about whether anyone still knows the difference between right and wrong.

Along with the new humanism, there is also an increasing cultural radicalism. Lasch, writing like an ancient prophet, argues that a once rugged and resourceful nation is now seething with a destructive rage, masquerading as the pleasure principle:

Having overthrown feudalism and slavery and then out-grown its own personal and familiar form, capitalism has evolved a new political ideology, welfare liberalism, which absolves individuals of moral responsibility and treats them as victims of social circumstance. It has evolved new modes of social control, which deal with the deviant as a patient and substitute medical rehabilitation for punishment. It has given rise to a new culture, the narcissistic culture of our time.[10]

Scientifically, Man Refuses to Acknowledge the Cause or Even the Reality of the Problem

If there is no God—and of course then that "non-god" was never involved in a personal creation—then man has no responsibility to Him, because a non-being could hardly be self-revealed as the Christian claims. The bleak, dark conclusion which logically awaits anyone willing to travel the total road of evolution is spelled out by Jacques Monod. Man is alone in a universe of "unfeeling immensity" in which he arrived by chance. And arriving by chance he may as well give up idle dreams of having a "destiny." There is no destiny. There is no purpose. There is no significance. And therefore there are no laws, no duty, and no morality.[11]

But Skinner hastens to attempt a rescue of such despair. Yes, contemporary man is a mechanical being stripped of freedom and dignity, but the personality can be designed and engineered from the outside by an intricate system of social pressures, he states. People cannot handle the problems around them because they have not developed as fast as technology, so they must turn the technology on themselves and use social engineering to manipulate human behavior. But who writes the prescriptions and pushes the buttons? Or to put it another way, who engineers the engineers? Skinner has a simple answer—"Trust me."

We wish we could. Skinner pleads his case well. But

there is that little slip twixt the cup and the lip that holds us back. There is danger here, for Skinner's social engineer has a completely different idea about what people are. We are machines. We do not have a divine origin. Our nature is caused entirely by our environment. If one wants to change what we are, one simply changes our environment. There is no definition for human. We are what we make ourselves—no, not even that—we are what our environment makes of us. We are pawns.[12]

If Skinner cannot be trusted, is there no hope in the scientific community? It is interesting that more and more scientists are beginning to question the hypothesis of animalistic evolution in their search for new meaning. Max Planck openly admitted the limitations of science:

> But there is another, far broader law, which has the property of giving a specific, unequivocal answer to each and every sensible question concerning the course of a natural process . . . but what we must regard as the greatest wonder of all is the fact that the most adequate formulation of this law creates the impression in every unbiased mind that nature is ruled by a rational, purposive will.[13]

Even three years before Planck's important article, E.F. Caldin in another article questioned the authority of science as a determiner of truth:

> Science, then, is not an adequate description of nature: it is a portrait made by an observer with a particular point of view and a definite limitation of his vision; from natural science we cannot learn what material nature is for, how and why it exists at all, and why it has any laws. . . . Science by itself throws no light on its own value, nor on values in general. It is not a royal road to knowledge of every kind.[14]

DELINEATION OF THE SOLUTION

More people are recognizing a "rational, purposive will" behind the cosmos. However, many make religion subject to science. What is the solution to moral entropy? Who will win the battle for the mind? Look with me at a brief history of how people have struggled with this problem.

The Medieval Synthesis: Tradition and Reason

In the Middle Ages, Thomas Aquinas reconstructed ideas from Augustine of Hippo:

> When the city of Rome was being overwhelmed by barbarian hordes under Alaric in A.D. 410 and it seemed to thinking people that civilization was coming to an end, that total chaos would ensue, that all hopes of progress and orderly living were to cease, then Augustine, building upon the writings of his predecessors but illuminating them enormously from his own giant intellect, bequeathed to the world between A.D. 414 and 426 his own contribution, *The City of God.* Here he endeavored to assure his readers that there is still meaning and purpose in it all, that God is still the great planner, and that though events in the earthly sphere seem to be completely without reason or order or hope, in the spiritual realm God remains in sovereign control, and world history is moving exactly as He intends it to.[15]

Augustine was primarily concerned with the relationships between man and God, man and nature, man and sin, God and nature, and man and society. Through the Dark Ages these ideas were retained (though at times in a most fragmented and inconspicuous form) until Aquinas reconstructed the thesis into an elaborate and logical worldview which has been called "the medieval synthesis."

Whether or not one agrees with the medieval synthesis, one

27

must admit that it was an orderly package, a worldview that linked the supernatural with the natural and promoted a unity of purpose with religious zeal.

> In this medieval synthesis, every line of thought and study was integrated with one objective ideally in view, which was to clothe the mind of man with the garment of understanding that would enable him to come humbly but with assurance into the presence of God and worship Him knowingly, recognizing the extent of his responsibilities and accepting his position in the economy of things with proper dignity, and—so they supposed—having also a full understanding of God's thoughts. I say "ideally," because it has to be admitted that this high aim of education was often replaced by the much lower one of maintaining the status quo.[16]

The Modern Synthesis: Science and Reason

In the Renaissance the marriage of science and religion entered the divorce court of the new learning as the purpose of education increasingly became the emancipation of man rather than the worship of God. Historian Kenneth Walker comments on this development:

> When we trace the history of theology and science . . . we find that they slowly diverged from each other and in the course of time became isolated departments of knowledge expressing contradictory views of the universe. As Hardwick has pointed out, the human mind has a faculty of creating prisms for itself, and eventually the scientific spirit incarcerated itself in a materialistic scheme of the universe which completely cut it off not only from religion but from all fruitful speculation concerning man's nature. In like manner, the self-sufficient pedantry of the church scholars had the effect of enclosing religion in a rigid casing of thought, which completely

isolated it from all the new discoveries being made by the scientists. Insulated from each other's ideas and pitifully satisfied with the sufficiency of their respective beliefs, it was inevitable that in the end scientists and teachers of religion should come into conflict.[17]

So reason, happily wed in the days of Aquinas to tradition and religion, now flirts with the new girl on the block—science—and though a formal wedding was never held, they immediately began to live together.

The compromise with religion seems to be very desirable; under the modern synthesis Robert Jastrow, director of NASA's Goddard Institute for Space Studies and professor of astronomy at Columbia University, offers a "new Book of Genesis" based on the "big bang theory":

> Now we see how the astronomical evidence leads to a biblical view of the origin of the world. The details differ, but the essential elements in the astronomical and biblical accounts of Genesis are the same: The chain of events leading to man commenced suddenly and sharply at a definite moment in time, in a flash of light and energy.[18]

The Miracle Synthesis: Revelation and Reason

Neither the medieval synthesis nor the modern synthesis satisfies the claims of evangelical Christianity. A third alternative could also be called "The Message Synthesis" with a focus on the self-revealed God, "The Master Synthesis" with a focus on the lordship of Christ, "The Mystery Synthesis" with a focus on the unveiling of the gospel in the New Testament, or "The Meaning Synthesis," since it alone among all the philosophies of modern man offers genuine rationality for time and eternity.

But the word *miracle* is chosen because that is precisely what Creation was. The God who formed man is the same God who reforms man, and therefore the revelation of regeneration provides the only answer to the world's dilemma.

In the miracle of creation, God made man. In the miracle of the Incarnation, He gave man the God-man. And in the miracle of regeneration, He restores man to Himself.

What is a miracle? Custance gives this clear definition: "I believe that miracles are occasions upon which God suspends or supersedes or accelerates or in some way modifies the natural order so that an event occurs which is entirely exceptional. A miracle then, according to this view, would be an indication that God is interfering in the natural order by an act of will because it pleases Him to do so."[19]

The God of miracles created the unfriendly porcupine which can carry up to 30,000 quills to repel its predators. Though exclusively a defensive animal, the porcupine is a killer since a fox or timber wolf might die of starvation, unable to eat because of the quills in its mouth. It is said that only one North American animal can kill a porcupine with impunity—a large member of the weasel family called the "fisher," which has developed a knack of flipping porcupines over on their backs and attacking the unprotected underside. Why should one creature alone be able to do this? It is one of the mysteries in the endless fascination of the God of creation.

The flight of wild geese is a study in aerodynamics. The leader of the "V" formation breaks trail through the air, and each bird thereafter gains "lift" from the updraft created by the wing action of the one in front of it. Being the leader is not easy, and that is why one can see the birds change the lead position periodically, as if by prearrangement. It all works so smoothly that spectators rarely stop to ponder what a remarkable system it is.[20]

The God of the porcupine, the weasel, and the goose seeks to transform the mind of man so that through the haze of sin which surrounds him he can see again the purity of the Creator. Paul wrote, "Do not conform any longer to the pattern of this world, but be transformed by the renewing of your mind. Then you will be able to test and approve what God's will is— His good, pleasing, and perfect will" (Rom. 12:2). The word for "mind" here is also found in Romans 14:5, 2 Thessalonians

2:2, and 1 Corinthians 2:16 (where the same apostle says to believers, "But we have the mind of Christ").

So how should Christians press the battle for the mind? What practical solutions are there in combating the black plague of sin in heart, home, and humanity? Here are three suggestions.

Declare war on theological ignorance. That is what Paul did in Athens when he proclaimed a real God in place of an unknown one (Acts 17:22-23). Nothing is to be gained by ignoring the theological dimensions of the creation conflict. In the final analysis, the issue is theological, not scientific. Either God said what He meant and meant what He said, or the entire message of redemption is unreliable. Sometimes people are lulled into comfort by the ignorance of their own limited worlds, somewhat like the little girl who was asked by her grandmother why she never cried in the dark at home but always did so at grandmother's house. The child replied, "But, Grandma, at home it's my own darkness."

Declare war on theological indifference. Too many believers are careless about the accuracy of their theology. They have no time for the exegesis and exposition which lays the groundwork for theological and philosophical systems. In one sense, such indifference is just another form of ignorance. Cornelius Jaarsma attacked it over three decades ago:

> Faith is not the asylum of ignorance to which are assigned the things we believe but do not understand. Nor is faith the sphere of religion, and reason or understanding the sphere of knowledge. Neither is faith based on reason in the sense that we believe a thing true or false because we understand it. The Christian faith is the source of knowledge which is basic to the true understanding of all things experienced.[21]

Declare war on theological intellectualism. Theological intellectualism is that snobbery of contemporary existential religion which accepts Jastrow's "new Genesis" as a happy compromise, thereby throwing man back into the pit of modern synthesis. One wonders whether there is more danger in intellectualism or ignorance, for like choosing "tails" on a two-headed coin, one loses whichever way it falls.

Of course, attacking intellectualism does not mean declaring war on intellect. The believer is to offer his renewed and dedicated mind as a sacrifice to God. In response to Monod's mournful wail of no destiny, contemporary Christian poet Joe Parks has written "Destiny":

Before the worlds were made
Or stars above displayed
A loving God had made a great design.
Before the planets flew
Or earth broke into view
Their form was fashioned in the Master's mind.
Now we can see that from Eternity
His perfect wisdom carried out a plan.
And we are all a part
Of what was in His heart
The moment when He first created man.[22]

NOTES

1. Francis A. Schaeffer, *No Final Conflict* (Downers Grove, Ill.: InterVarsity Press, 1975), 18.
2. Matthew 19:4-5; 24:37-39; Mark 10:6; Luke 3:38; 17:26-27; Romans 5:12; 1 Corinthians 6:16; 11:8-9,12; 15:21-22,45; 2 Corinthians 11:3; Ephesians 5:31; 1 Timothy 2:13-14; Hebrews 11:7; 1 Peter 3:20; 2 Peter 2:5; 3:4-6; 1 John 3:12; Jude 11:14; Revelation 14:7.
3. James Oliver Buswell, *A Systematic Theology of the Christian Religion,* 2 vols. (Grand Rapids: Zondervan Publishing House, 1962), 1:298.
4. Ibid., 256.
5. Ibid., 259.
6. Karl Menninger, *Whatever Became of Sin?* (New York: Hawthorne, 1973).

7. Carl F. Henry, *Twilight of a Great Civilization* (Westchester, Ill.: Crossway Books, 1988), 21.

8. Thomas Howard, "The Touchstone," *Christianity Today*, 5 January 1979, 12.

9. Kenneth Boulding, *The Meaning of the 20th Century* (New York: Harper & Row, 1964).

10. Christopher Lasch, *The Culture of Narcissism: American Life in an Age of Diminishing Expectations* (New York: Northon, 1978).

11. Jacques Monod, *Chance and Necessity* (New York: A. Knopf, 1971), 180.

12. Nancy B. Barcus, *Developing a Christian Mind* (Downers Grove, Ill.: InterVarsity Press, 1977), 80.

13. Max Planck, "Religion and Natural Science," *Scientific Autobiography and Other Writings* (New York: Philosophical Library, 1949), 184.

14. E. F. Caldin, "Value and Science," *Endeavour*, October 1946, 161.

15. Arthur C. Custance, *Science and Faith*, The Doorway Papers, vol. 8 (Grand Rapids: Zondervan Publishing House, 1978), 109.

16. Ibid., 112.

17. Kenneth Walker, *Meaning and Purpose* (London: Pelican Books, 1944), 28.

18. Robert Jastrow, "A New Genesis," *Miami Herald*, 22 October 1978, E1.

19. Custance, *Science and Faith*, 208.

20. "A Knowledge of Nature," *The Royal Bank of Canada Monthly Letter*, July 1978, 3.

21. Cornelius Jaarsma, "Christian Theism and the Empirical Sciences," *Monograph of the American Scientific Affiliation* (August 1947): 71.

22. Joe E. Parks, *Destiny* (Grand Rapids: Singspiration, 1971).

3

WHAT IS BEHIND MORALITY?
Kenneth D. Boa

Morality is universal. Whether a person is a philosopher or a theologian, a poet or a scientist, the experiences he has during his lifetime are somehow similar to those of other individuals.

No matter what their culture, people have moral experiences, aesthetic experiences, and religious experiences. The idea of right versus wrong and good versus bad is firmly entrenched in the human mind, and it is consistently displayed in the human experience. The norms of morality may vary, but all people tend to believe that some things are right and some things are wrong. Even for those who claim that there is really no such thing as what they would call right or wrong, every time they criticize, applaud, approve, or accuse, they implicitly appeal to some fixed standard of right and wrong.

There are variations, contradictions, and even absurdities among the ethical codes in various parts of the world. But all too often, the differences and contradictions are emphasized so much that the overwhelming number of similarities is neglected. These similarities are so extensive that they point to a "traditional morality" or "natural law" which has been derived from human experience in all ages and countries. There is, for example, a principle of general beneficence to mankind which is clearly articulated in the moral codes of China, Babylon, Egypt, India, Israel, Rome, and elsewhere. In all societies the principles of fairness, kindness, and honesty toward other people can be found. Moral codes from cultures around the world emphasize duties toward parents, elders, and ancestors on the one hand, and toward children and posterity on the other. Furthermore, there is a universal admiration of the qualities of generosity, mercy, wisdom, courage, self-control, and patience.

These traditional moral principles make up an ethical standard which has been given various names. In India it has been called the *dharma* or the *rita*. In China it was called the *tao*, the "way" of the universe which should be imitated by man. This moral law allows for modifications and developments, and this explains some of the differences among ethical codes. But as C.S. Lewis argues, the development must be from within.[1] One cannot cogently contend for a new ethical code by stepping entirely outside the boundary of traditional morality. If he makes any appeal for the validity of his ethical system, it will necessarily be a masked appeal to those moral principles which are already evident in the moral law.

Therefore, philosophers and religious leaders have been able to clarify and bring about advances in the principles of traditional morality, but no one has instituted an entirely new moral value for the world to behold. There is no question that the Golden Rule as set forth by Christ ("In everything, do to others what you would have them do to you," Matt. 7:12) is an advancement over the Silver Rule of Confucius ("What you do not want done to yourself, do not do to others," Analects 15:23). But it is not a radically new value. As Lewis says, "The human mind has no more power of inventing a new value than of imagining a new primary color, or, indeed, of creating a new sun and a new sky for it to move in."[2]

Many attempts have been made in recent years to arrive at new moralities by abandoning traditional values. But those who do so generally eliminate the bulk of these values while clinging tenaciously to the few they have decided to keep. To illustrate, a number of people today endeavor to reduce their ethical system to the maxim, "Do your own thing as long as it doesn't interfere with others." Far from being a new morality, however, this would be better described as a severely truncated version of the traditional morality. It really represents an arbitrary choice of one maxim from a number of maxims, and there is no logically consistent basis for choosing this particular one and eliminating the rest. It reduces to a subjective (and inadequate) moral code. The same is true for those who scoff at traditional moral values and claim that the only moral imperative people should be concerned about in modern culture is the "good of society" or the "survival of the species." The only real basis for these moral values is the traditional moral law from which they are derived, though this is the very thing these people are attempting to jettison.

But what is the basis for the traditional moral law? If these values are based solely on human experiences and subjective feelings, there is a real problem. When people criticize or appeal to moral values, they are appealing to something which in their minds is self-evident and objective.

Jesus Himself did not institute an entirely new ethical code, even though He did bring about many refinements. Instead, He addressed those who admitted their sinfulness and disobedience to the already-known moral law. If moral principles were not accepted as self-evident, no one would have sensed his need for the redemption from sin which Jesus was offering.

Certain things must be regarded as given; otherwise nothing can be proved. The given in the area of morality is that something must be good or bad for its own sake. If someone says that the human race should be preserved and that we should be concerned about posterity, another might well ask him why this should be so. It would not require many of these whys before the former is forced to admit that the thing he desires is good because he believes it is good. Each person entertains the concept that some things are objectively right and other things are simply wrong. Even a naturalist who scornfully inveighs against the irrational prohibitions found in the traditional morality has moral values of his own in the background. The process of rationalizing and explaining things away has a definite limit. If it is carried too far, nothing (including explanation itself) will be left.

Thus it can be said that human moral experience points to certain things. It points to a set of transcultural and transtemporal moral values which are held to be self-evidently and objectively true. It shows that these values cannot be entirely overthrown despite many attempts to do so, because no one lives in a moral vacuum. Further, it shows that no one is able to introduce a radically new moral value.

All this leads to a serious problem. Human moral experience does not account for itself. Instead, it consistently appeals to the existence of some kind of objective standard for its validity. And the objective standard must be external to mankind rather than a subjective fabrication of human minds. Sartre stated that if a finite point does not have an infinite reference point, the finite point is absurd. Man is not his own God. The person who claims that man created God in his own image, for example, runs into trouble when it comes to moral judgments. In effect, he must reduce moral values to a subjective sentiment produced by cultural conditioning. And if this is so, what basis does he have for being outraged at the cruelties of racial hatred, of violent crime, or even of Hitler's Third Reich? Certainly he cannot say that any of these things are wrong or right in any objective and ultimate sense. For by his own admission he has diluted moral values to the level of pure relativism.

SEVERAL APPROACHES TO MORALITY

It is the thesis of this chapter that morality has no genuine validity unless it points to a higher dimension. In order to support this contention, it is necessary to look at the logical implications of several competing approaches. Two ingredients are essential: horizontal self-consistency and vertical fitting of the facts.[3] An ethical system must first be logically consistent; its terms must obey the law of contradiction. Second, it must fit with the facts of the real world. One of the principal non-facts it must reckon with is man's cruelty and his egotistic nature. It must also provide a means of harnessing human desires to carry out this duty. Duty and desire must somehow be merged.

Skepticism

The first basic approach to the problem of ethics is that of total skepticism. This says that there is no rational answer for anything that exists. The universe is meaningless and absurd. Life has no real meaning, and death is the greatest absurdity of all. A number of existentialists have arrived at this position, and it is also the theme of many books, plays, and films. According to this viewpoint, there is no basis at all for moral values. Carried far enough on a theoretical level, it would mean that a person could kill or be kind to another person, and it would make no ultimate difference.

This approach cannot be maintained by anyone on a practical level. No one can be consistent with a position of complete skepticism. There is form and order in the world, and people live each day as though this were true, whether they admit it or not. They communicate with others in very rational ways and make hundreds of choices which presuppose a consistent and orderly environment.

Naturalism

Another basic approach to ethics is found in naturalism. Naturalism takes many forms, but all of them assign an impersonal beginning to the universe. The universe and all the phenomena in it are the products of the laws of nature plus time and chance. Naturalism has no place for a personal or supernatural agent at work in originating and sustaining the universe. So the naturalist looks to utility, to instinct, or to reason as his source for moral values.

This approach is inadequate for several reasons. One problem is that it gives no meaning for the particulars of nature and

LIVING ETHICALLY IN THE '90s

2 3 4 5 6 7 8 9 10 Printing / Year 94 93 92 91 90

for mankind. Man has no significance or value in an impersonal universe. Such a universe would have no ordering agency, and it would not account for the complexity observed in living systems. Moreover, it does not explain the personality of man. Personality (including intellect, emotion, and will) is on a higher order than impersonality, and yet the naturalist maintains that it is a product of impersonal, chance factors. However, reason and experience consistently show that no effect can be greater than its cause. Personality cannot be derived from an entirely impersonal basis.

Man's rational mind is one aspect of his personality. And it is here that naturalism runs into another impasse. Naturalistic theories teach in effect that the human mind is the chance byproduct of an irrational and mindless process. This means that carried to its logical conclusion, the natural evolutionary theory strips away the basis for rationality itself. It reduces human reason to biochemical and electrical mechanisms. Those who argue that man's thoughts can be fully explained as the result of irrational causes are in reality attempting to prove that there are no such things as proofs. It is a self-defeating process to use human reason to call into question the validity of human reason. There can be no knowledge at all unless certain basic things are assumed to be true. All scientists build their work, for example, on at least three presuppositions: (1) The universe is orderly; (2) Men will be honest in their research methods and reports; and (3) Knowledge is possible. All these presuppositions require a rationality behind the universe.

As stated earlier, the naturalist hopes to find his moral values in utility, in instinct, or in reason. However, none of these is sufficient to generate valid judgments of value. Neither utility (the usefulness of an act for a community) nor instinct can provide a logically consistent basis for one willingly to sacrifice his life for the sake of others. Scientific humanists often speak approvingly about the human instinct for the preservation of the species. They use this as the foundation for the moral imperative that people should live and work for posterity. But in so doing, they ignore several fatal difficulties. Man has a number of instincts or natural desires, but they are not all harmonious. They are struggling against one another, vying for man's attention. The satisfaction of one (e.g., the preservation of the species) can mean the deprivation of others (e.g., the preservation of one's own life). Whence comes the imperative that an instinct like the preservation of humanity should be placed above man's other instincts? There is no ground in naturalism for saying that it is more fundamental or basic than the others. Why should a person obey one instinct and control others?

Humans have a natural impulse to preserve their own lives and the lives of their children. But this impulse becomes weaker and more abstract the further it is projected into the future. Humans are far more concerned with the well-being of their children and grandchildren than they are with their descendants a thousand years hence. Thus for one to risk his life or the lives of his children for the sake of an abstract posterity has no instinctual foundation at all. Besides this, the sacrifice of one's life would frustrate the satisfaction of every other drive he has.

When one comes right down to it, the naturalist's imperative of the preservation of humanity is not after all based on instinct but on an ethical maxim derived from traditional morality.

The same is true of attempts to base morality on pure reason. Reason alone is not sufficient to lead from a statement in the indicative ("this is so") to a statement such as "this ought to be so," or "we should do this." It is necessary to assume the ethical from the beginning in order to move from an "is" to an "ought."[4]

Humanism

The humanist offers another approach. He says that man should be his own lawmaker; he can create his own values. For the humanist, man takes the place of God and eliminates the need for a transcendent realm.

One option within humanism is individualistic ethics. In this case every person should do "that which is right in his own eyes." However, when everything is regarded from one's own experiences, feelings, and desires, anarchy rather than morality is produced.

Group ethics is a second option. The problem here is that groups and societies can pursue paths as evil as those followed by any individual. Societies are concerned only for their own good and often try to achieve it at the expense of others. Instead of every man for himself, this is a case of every nation for itself.[5]

The third option within humanism seeks to find universal principles of conduct which transcend personal or group barriers. The brotherhood of all men and the need to respect the lives and needs of others are usually mentioned in this connection.

As good as this sounds, humanism provides no philosophical basis for values like these. It offers only an impersonal beginning to the universe. Man is just a by-product of a slow evolutionary process. Since everything is relative, there are no true morals or absolute standards. Man is left with changing majority values and arbitrary sociological standards. There is no way of being sure that any of today's cherished ethical values will be valid tomorrow. If man is cruel, it is simply part of his nature. Humanism is unable to take an absolute stand against the many examples of attempted genocide in the 20th century because it has no absolutes to which it can appeal. The humanist cannot establish ethical criteria that are universally normative. The humanist position leads to skepticism not only about moral values, but also about the dignity of man. Humanity is just a minute and ephemeral accident in an impersonal and dying cosmos.

Pantheism

Instead of deifying man, others have opted to deify the universe. This is the pantheistic approach. Pantheism, like naturalism and humanism, is unable to create a foundation for morality, because according to it the universe is everything, and everything is the universe.

Pantheism allows man to have no moral categories because what he calls right and wrong are simply reducible to a part of all that is. There is no ultimate difference between love and hate or between good and evil.

THEISM'S APPROACH TO MORALITY

It is evident that the views of skepticism, naturalism, humanism, and pantheism all fall short of providing man with an adequate basis for moral values. None of them really takes man above de Sade's dictum, "What is, is right." Because of their relativism, these systems are unable to offer a valid answer to the question, Why is murder wrong? Among the plethora of "sophisticated" pornographic films is a film which depicts death by strangulation as a final part of the "love act." Many advocates of the approaches considered thus far would no doubt feel that there is something wrong with a film like this, but can they prove it according to the premises of their systems? What can they really say about the increasing dehumanization of man in today's technological age? They may criticize wars and racial prejudice and cruelty, but in so doing they are appealing to objective and absolute standards of value which they do not acknowledge.

Unlike these other approaches, theism proposes a personal beginning to the universe. Man is the product of an intelligent and personal ordering-agent rather than an impersonal and mindless cosmos. This means that there is a rational mind which in turn produced the human mind. There is a sufficient basis behind human rationality.

In order for the God of theism to have created this universe, He must be infinite as well as personal. He is the ultimate whose character provides the absolute standard for morality. To speak of true moral values, one must no longer regard man's conscience as a by-product of nature. Rather, it

WHAT IS BEHIND MORALITY?

must be derived from a source which is absolutely moral. Nature itself is not rational or moral, but its Creator is.

When people appeal to standards of morality which they believe are objective and absolute, they are living (whether they admit it or not) as though theism were true. Their moral behavior presupposes a transcendent absolute. If God is to be a sufficient integration point for man, He must be infinite, personal, rational, and good. Psalm 19:1-6 and Romans 1:20 say that the creation is able to tell man certain things about the Creator, including His intelligence, His eternal power, and His divine nature.

Nevertheless, this kind of natural revelation has definite limits. If man is left only to his religious experiences, he will have little authority to say much more than this about God. Religious experience is interpreted in radically different ways, and the resulting concepts of God are often mutually exclusive.

The Bible, however, claims to be God's authoritative revelation to man. It says that God is not only transcendent; He is also immanent. Instead of being silent, He has communicated to man. The One who created space and time entered into His own creation as the God-man in order to "give His life a ransom for many" (Mark 10:45). Because of God's revelation to us, our concept of God need not be limited to a fabrication of our own minds.

According to the Scriptures, the traditional moral values discussed earlier are a result of the image of God in us. God has implanted the moral law in the human conscience to the extent that those who are honest with themselves must admit that they are unable consistently to live up to the standards they intuitively believe are right. "Indeed, when Gentiles, who do not have the law, do by nature things required by the law, they are a law for themselves, even though they do not have the law, since they show that the requirements of the law are written on their hearts, their consciences also bearing witness, and their thoughts now accusing, now even defending them" (Rom. 2:14-15). This is why human moral experience leads to certain values which transcend cultural and temporal barriers.

43

God did not create standards of morality or goodness. Neither does He obey them. Absolute goodness was never created, because it is God's eternal character. God revealed His character in the Old and New Testaments, and the God-man Jesus Christ perfectly lived it before men. God's character is above time and space; in it is a changeless criterion for right and wrong. This provides an absolute basis for morality.

Nevertheless there is still a problem when one speaks of the goodness of God, and this is the existence of evil in the world. Briefly, the biblical explanation of this problem is that the creature, not God, is responsible for the sin and sorrow of natural and moral evil. Because of the Fall of man, nature was also cursed. This is the origin of the natural disease-death environment. The Bible speaks of a time when nature, like man, will be resurrected from its slavery to corruption (e.g., Rom. 8:19-22). Death itself will be overcome. "For since death came through a man the resurrection of the dead came also through a man. For as in Adam all die, so in Christ all will be made alive" (1 Cor. 15:21-22, NASB). Man as he is now is not what he was when God created him. Man has not always been cruel. The Scriptures reveal that he changed himself in his rebellion against God from his original state of sinlessness to his present condition. There is now a moral discontinuity in man. Each person knows things about himself that he would not dare tell others. People cannot even criticize others without condemning themselves because they often find themselves guilty of practicing the same things. Mankind has abused every good gift God has given it including nature, authority, sex, marriage, food, and wealth.

God created man, but He did not cause him to sin. Sin by definition is that which is contrary to the character of God. To create a sinful state of affairs God would have to rebel against Himself. And yet many have contended that God's standard of goodness in the Bible is contrary to man's social standards of goodness. John Stuart Mill held this position. More recently, Ayn Rand went a step further and assailed the whole concept of God as "morally evil."[6] However, this ignores the fact that

44

human morality, if it is to have any ultimate validity, must be derived from an absolute, and therefore external, base. C.S. Lewis argues for this point:

> There is, to be sure, one glaringly obvious ground for denying that any moral purpose at all is operative in the universe: namely, the actual course of events in all its wasteful cruelty and apparent indifference, or hostility, to life. But then, as I maintain, that is precisely the ground which we cannot use. Unless we judge this waste and cruelty to be real evils, we cannot of course condemn the universe for exhibiting them. Unless we take our own standard of goodness to be valid in principle (however fallible our particular applications of it) we cannot mean anything by calling waste and cruelty evils. And unless we take our own standard to be something more than ours, to be in fact an objective principle to which we are responding, we cannot regard that standard as valid. In a word, unless we allow ultimate reality to be moral, we cannot morally condemn it.[7]

If morality is to rise above the subjective sentiments and opinions of finite creatures, there must be an ultimate authority whose eternal character is the essence of goodness, truth, and love. Two important conclusions follow from all this: (1) God is not responsible for the origin of evil, and (2) His character is the absolute upon which morality must be based. The Bible reveals God's character and it also shows that all men have true moral guilt—they fall short of God's standard. However, the Bible also reveals that God Himself has provided a solution to man's moral dilemma through the substitutionary work of Christ. He offers release from sin's dominion and provides a way of reconciliation with the holy God.

Christian theism unites duty and desire. The duty consists of a right relation to God and (consequently) a right relation to humanity. And Christ gives us a reason for carrying out this duty. He provides peace, security, joy, and a new quality of life to those who trust in Him. Thus the religious life and the moral life converge in a relationship with Jesus Christ. A genuine Christian does not regard God as an abstract concept or an impersonal Absolute. Instead, the believer desires to lead a life which is pleasing to God (i.e., a moral life) as part of his gratitude and love for the God who first loved him: "This is love: not that we loved God, but that He loved us and sent His Son as an atoning sacrifice for our sins. Dear friends, since God so loved us, we also ought to love one another" (1 John 4:10-11). Christians are to love God in response to His love for them, and they are to love each other as a result of their love for God.[8] "We love because He first loved us. If anyone says, 'I love God,' yet hates his brother, he is a liar. For anyone who does not love his brother whom he has seen, cannot love God whom he has not seen. And He has given us this command: Whoever loves God must also love his brother" (1 John 4:19-21, NASB).

NOTES

1. C.S. Lewis, *The Abolition of Man* (New York: Macmillan Co., 1947) and some of his essays in *Christian Reflections*, ed. Walter Hooper (Grand Rapids: Wm. B. Eerdmans Publishing Co., 1967).

2. Lewis, *Abolition of Man*, 56-57.

3. Edward J. Carnell, *An Introduction to Christian Apologetics* (Grand Rapids: Wm. B. Eerdmans Publishing Co., 1948), 316–18.

4. Henry B. Veatch, *Two Logics* (Evanston, Ill.: Northwestern University Press, 1969), 252.

5. Carnell, *Christian Apologetics*, 326.

6. See Barbara Branden, *Who Is Ayn Rand?* (New York: Random House, 1962); 162. In her philosophy of objectivism, Rand sought to replace altruism with "creative selfishness" (Charles F. Schroder, "Ayn Rand: Far Right Prophetess," *Christian Century*, 13 December 1961, 1943).

7. Lewis, *Christian Reflections*, 69–70.

8. Joseph Fletcher, Bishop John Robinson, and others have attempted to arrive at a morality which replaces an absolute standard with "love." Fletcher's *Situation Ethics* uses a number of Christian

terms, but his system is far removed from biblical Christianity. The Scriptures also emphasize love, but not to the exclusion of God's moral law. Though Fletcher claims that love is the fundamental principle which should determine man's behavior, he is blatantly inconsistent in his definition of this crucial word. Sometimes it means a motive, sometimes an action, and sometimes a formal principle. He is also inconsistent in his analysis of what makes an act moral; is it the act itself, the intentions behind the act, or the consequences of the act? Because of this confusion about the meaning of love and the meaning of morality, situationism is of no practical use as an ethical system. It leads directly to personal preferences and ethical subjectivity. The word *love* is given no real content, and situationism offers no workable rules for loving actions. Both ends and means are relative, and situation ethics has no basis for elevating love from a relative to an absolute plane. A system founded on relativism cannot logically appeal to an unchanging absolute.

4

HOMOSEXUALITY AND THE BIBLE

P. Michael Ukleja

od loves people and wants them to come to the whole-
ness and joy for which they were made. His prohibitions
are not the house rules of a sadistic and capricious Deity
who mocks people by tormenting them with desires and then
forbidding them from doing anything about them. Biblical prohibitions are bright signposts that point people straight toward
fullness and joy. They warn people away from spiritual and
emotional detours, mires, quicksand, and cliffs. They are not
in the least ambiguous about the quicksand of homosexuality.

All sexual sins represent some failure on society's part to
stick to God's path. Fornication fails to honor the image of God
in the other person, for it sees the other only as a commodity.
Adultery violates the shrine of marital fidelity which houses
and keeps sacred the sexual expression. Incest is the effort to
achieve union with an image too close to oneself. The relationship is not sufficiently "other" to make the transaction valid.
Bestiality is the effort to achieve union with an image too
different from oneself. Masturbation, while not explicitly cited
in Scripture as sin, involves a failure to appreciate fully the use
of sex which is surely more than a matter of mere orgasm.
And homosexuality is a confusion, since it involves the effort of
achieving union with a "mirror" image of oneself. This "other"
is not sufficiently different to permit the union for which mankind was so remarkably formed.

HOMOSEXUALITY AND THE SIN OF SODOM

Two angels who came to Lot in Sodom were threatened by a mob (Gen. 19:4-11). What were the men of Sodom seeking when they called on Lot to bring out the men "that we may know them" (19:5, KJV)?

Some believe that the story has no reference to homosexual acts at all. Bailey seeks to justify homosexuality from the Old Testament in his work *Homosexuality and the Western Christian Tradition*.[1] Others (e.g., Boswell[2]) use Bailey's arguments concerning this passage. Bailey was an Anglican scholar whose work influenced the change in British law regarding this issue. This work is fast becoming a standard reference work for the pro-homosexuality viewpoint.

Bailey believes that much of Christian prejudice against homosexuality is the result of misunderstanding the story of Sodom in Genesis 19. He argues that the men of Sodom were anxious to interrogate the strangers to find out if they were spies. Therefore, he argues, the story does not refer to homosexuality at all. The sin involved was not homosexuality, but gang rape. Lot had angered these residents by receiving foreigners whose credentials had not been examined. The men were angered by this omission, and were showing extreme discourtesy to these visitors by demanding to know their credentials.[3] Bailey argues that the demand of the men of Sodom to "know" the strangers in Lot's house meant nothing more than their desire to "get acquainted with" them. The problem, argues Bailey, was nothing more than inhospitality. Others, including Blair, have expanded on this argument.

The biblical story demonstrates the seriousness with which these early Eastern people took the important customs of Oriental hospitality. It appears that, if necessary, they would even allow their own daughters to undergo abuse in order to protect guests. The sexual aspect of the story is simply the vehicle in which the subject of demanded hospitality is conveyed. It is clearly interpreted in Ezekiel 16:49: "Behold, this was the guilt of your sister Sodom: she and her daughters had pride, surfeit of food, and prosperous ease, but did not aid the poor and needy."[4]

The Hebrew word for "know," Bailey points out, can be translated "to get acquainted with" or "to have knowledge of" or "to have intercourse with." The word appears over 943 times in the Old Testament and only 12 times does it mean "to have intercourse with." He also states that intercourse, as a means to personal knowledge, depends on more than copulation. Therefore, he argues, the circumstances in Sodom could not fit the sexual connotation of the word *know*. He concludes by reasoning from the fact that Lot was a resident foreigner. As such, Lot had exceeded his rights by receiving two foreigners whose credentials had not been examined.[5]

A problem with this argument is the fact that the meaning of a word in a given passage is not determined solely on the basis of the number of times it is translated that way in the Bible. The context determines how it is to be translated. Of the 12 times the word "to know" occurs in Genesis, 10 times it means "to have intercourse with." Kidner offers the following rebuttal to Bailey's arguments:

> To this we may reply: (a) Statistics are no substitute for contextual evidence (otherwise the rarer sense of the word would never seem probable), and in both these passages the demand to "know" is used in its sexual sense (Gen. 19:8; Jud. 19:25). Even apart from this verbal conjunction it would be grotesquely inconsequent that Lot should reply to a demand for credentials by an offer of daughters. (b) Psychology can suggest how "to know" acquired its secondary sense; but in fact the use of the word is completely flexible. No one suggests that in Judges 19:25 the men of Gibeah were gaining "knowledge" of their victim in the sense of personal relationship, yet *know* is the word used of them. (c) Conjecture here

has the marks of special pleading for it substitutes a trivial reason ("commotion . . . in hospitality") for a serious one for the angels' decision. Apart from this, it is silenced by Jude 7, a pronouncement which Dr. Bailey has to discount as belonging to a late stage of interpretation.[6]

The whole scene in Genesis 19 takes on near-comic proportions if Lot, on hearing the demand of the crowd that they wished to "get acquainted with" the men in his house, said, "Please, my brothers, do not act wickedly. Now behold, I have two daughters who have not known a man; please let me bring them out to you and do to them as is good in your sight, only do nothing to these men" (author's translation). In verse 8 the same verb with the negative particle is used to describe Lot's daughters as having "not known" a man. The verb here obviously means "have intercourse with." It could hardly mean simply "be acquainted with." In narrative literature of this sort, it would be very unlikely to use one verb with two different meanings so close together unless the author made the difference quite obvious. In both verses 5 and 8, therfore, "to know" should be translated "to have sexual intercourse with." The context does not lend itself to any other credible interpretation.

Jude 7 gives a commentary on this passage. It clearly states that the sin of Sodom involved gross immorality and going after strange or different flesh. It is no accident that Jude describes their actions by using a word that definitely refers to sexual immorality, and the prepositional form explains that it means that "they gave themselves up fully, without reserve, thoroughly, out and out, utterly."[7] The term "strange flesh" could imply unnatural acts between men or even of human beings with animals. The inhabitants of Canaan were guilty of both of these sins (Lev. 18:23-29). This definitely includes the cities of Sodom and Gomorrah. History and archeology confirm these same conditions. Josephus, who wrote around A.D. 100, said that the Sodomites "hated strangers and abused themselves with sodomitical practices."[8]

Boswell says that Lot was following local customs in offering his daughters to appease the angry mob. "No doubt the surrender of his daughters was simply the most tempting bribe Lot could offer on the spur of the moment to appease the hostile crowd. . . . This action, almost unthinkable in modern Western society, was consonant with the very low status of female children at the time."⁹ But what Lot did was not right. The fact that Lot offered his daughters to them in accord with local customs does not mean that his action was morally acceptable in God's sight. It is much more probable that Lot's offer was motivated by the thought that however wrong rape is, homosexual rape was even worse. Lot's offer was simply what he thought to be the lesser of two evils.

HOMOSEXUALITY AND THE MOSAIC LAW

The Injunction in the Law

God's command concerning homosexuality is clear: "Do not lie with a man as one lies with a woman; that is detestable" (Lev. 18:22). This is expanded in Leviticus 20:13: "If a man lies with a man as one lies with a woman, both of them have done what is detestable." These passages are set in the context of God's judgment on sexual crimes and are an expansion of the seventh commandment, "You shall not commit adultery" (Ex. 20:14). The Mosaic law does not contain an exhaustive code on the subject of sexuality; rather, it deals with certain gross offenses of the seventh commandment that were common in the nations surrounding Israel at the time.

Homosexuality advocates usually dismiss these passages by relegating them to simple religious prohibitions rather than taking them as moral prohibitions. Blair exhibits this line of reasoning:

That the very pronounced Old Testament judgment against a man's having sexual relations with another man is included in the priestly holiness code of Leviticus (18:22 and 20:13) is significant because the concern of the priests was one of ritual purity. It was not the moral preaching of the prophets. From this priestly point of view, it is clear that above all else, Israel was to be uncontaminated by her pagan neighbors. In all things, she was to remain a separate "pure vessel unto the Lord." At this time, male prostitutes in the temples of the Canaanites, Babylonians, and other neighboring peoples were common features of the pagan rites. There, it is understandable that this "homosexuality" connected with the worship of false gods would certainly color Israel's perspective on any and all homosexual activity.[10]

Blair and those who follow his line of thinking assume that ritual purity and moral preaching are always distinct. Therefore they argue that the passages in Leviticus are not really speaking against homosexuality as such, but only against identifying with the practice of alien religions. The issue was religious identity, not the righteousness of God.

But this type of reasoning begs the question on several counts. The first major fault is in assuming that ritual purity and moral purity are always distinct. Those who make this dichotomy argue that Leviticus 18 and 20 cannot be of an ethical or moral nature. Blair states this when he divides the priests with their ritual purity and the prophets with their moral teaching into two groups that were not to transgress each other's territory. But the prophets preached to the needs of their day. Anything excluded from their teaching is more logically explained by that particular sin's absence among the sins of that generation, rather than by a rigid distinction between ceremonial and moral purity. To hold to such a distinction one would have to conclude that adultery was not morally wrong (18:20), child sacrifice had no moral implications (18:21), and that nothing is inherently evil with bestiality (18:23). The point is that ceremonial purity and moral purity often coincide.

These passages, again, are consistent with God's purpose for human sexuality. When these passages are studied, it becomes obvious that God's purpose is to preserve the sanctity of marriage and the home.

The Relevance of the Law

Homosexuality advocates spend much effort and time trying to show the irrelevance of Old Testament law to Christians today. Scanzoni and Mollenkott are an example of this: "Consistency and fairness would seem to dictate that if the Israelite Holiness Code is to be invoked against 20th-century homosexuals, it should likewise be invoked against such common practices as eating rare steak, wearing mixed fabrics, and having marital intercourse during the menstrual period."[11] Blair follows Scanzoni and Mollenkott in arguing that the Old Testament law must be thrown out when seeking a guide to the issue of homosexuality:

> It is interesting how lightly evangelicals have taken other proscriptions found in the same Old Testament code, e.g.: rules against the eating of rabbit (Lev. 11:26), oysters, clams, shrimp, and lobster (Lev. 11:10ff), and rare steaks (Lev. 17:10). Evangelicals do not picket or try to close down seafood restaurants, nor do we keep kosher kitchens. We do not always order steaks "well-done." We eat pork and ham. The wearing of clothes made from interwoven linen and wool (Deut. 22:11) does not seem to bother us at all. Evangelicals do not say, in accordance with these same laws of cultic purification (Lev. 20:13), that those who practice homosexual activity should be executed as prescribed. Evangelicals do not demand the death penalty for the Jeanne Dixons of this world (Lev. 20:27) nor do we "cut off" from among the people, as is demanded by this same code, those who have intercourse with women during menstruation (Lev. 20:18) and those who marry women who have been divorced (Lev.

21:14). Evangelicals do not keep out of the pulpit those who are visually handicapped or lame or those "with a limb too long" (Lev. 21:18ff).[12]

These statements expose a great ignorance of how the law fits into the total scheme of the Scriptures. When taken to their logical conclusion, these assertions make it possible to say that having sex with animals or engaging in incest is acceptable for today simply because homosexuality is sandwiched between these two prohibitions. These writers pay a great price in trying to justify their position. It would have been easier for them to say that Christ brought an end to the entire law (Rom. 10:4), including the Ten Commandments (2 Cor. 3:7-11). Christ is now the Christian's High Priest, which shows that a radical change in the law has come about (Heb. 7:11). The law has been superseded (7:11).

When the statement is made that the law had ended, this does not mean that God no longer has any laws or codes for His people. This does not mean that there are no moral precepts to be followed. The New Testament speaks of the "law of the Spirit" (Rom. 8:2), the "law of Christ" (Gal. 6:2), and the "royal law" (James 2:8). This "law" includes numerous commands, both positive and negative, which form a distinct code of ethics for today.[13] It is here that the pro-homosexuality exegetes have made their mistake. As a unit, the New Testament code is new, but not all the commands in the New Testament are new. There is overlap, deletion, and addition. Some of the commands in the Mosaic code have been incorporated into the New Testament code.

But if the law was done away, how can parts of it be repeated in the New Testament? The answer lies in the distinction between the Old Testament code and the commandments which were contained in that code.

The Mosaic law has been done away in its entirety as a code. God is no longer guiding the life of man by this particular code. In its place He has introduced the law of

Christ. Many of the individual commands within that law are new, but some are not. Some of the ones which are old were also found in the Mosaic law and they are now incorporated completely and forever done away. As part of the law of Christ they are binding on the believer today.[14]

This throws much light on the statements made by those who would justify homosexuality from a biblical standpoint. It serves to bring their emotional rhetoric into proper focus. The laws concerning diet, punishment by stoning, or wearing mixed fabrics have been abrogated. However, the proscriptions against homosexual behavior have been repeated in the New Testament code (Rom. 1:26-27; 1 Cor. 6:9-11; 1 Tim. 1:9-10). This should be a major concern of homosexuality advocates simply because it totally destroys the point they attempt to make with regard to the Old Testament law.

What this all means is that the commands dealing with homosexuality in Leviticus 18:23 and 20:13 are still highly relevant because they have been incorporated into the New Testament code. A moral unity exists between the Old and New Testaments. It has always been wrong to murder, rape, steal, to have sexual relations with animals or with persons of the same sex. God has dealt with people in different ways at different times, but His standard for righteousness has never changed. If morality has changed, then the character of God has changed, because the basis of morality is in the character of God who is immutable (Mal. 3:6).

PAUL'S TEACHING ON HOMOSEXUALITY

Several passages in the Pauline Epistles condemn homosexuality. Gay theology's major thrust against these passages is what has been called the "abuse argument." Justification for the practice of homosexuality is seen in interpreting Paul's condemnation to be against homosexual abuse and not against "responsible" homosexual behavior. Some argue that although this cannot be deduced, it is a strong inference. Blair writes:

In his catalog of vices in which homosexual behavior is listed, it should be noted that it is included with what the apostle regarded as certain heterosexual sins such as adultery, fornication, Epicurean overindulgence, and general abuse of the body. For perspective, note should be taken of Paul's equally weighty inclusion in this passage of drunkards and the repeated censure of the greedy, the grasping, and those who steal. Here are simply other examples of sinful abuse, since, for example, Paul advocated alcoholic temperance but not necessarily abstinence. He recommends to young Timothy that he drink some wine for his health (1 Tim. 5:23). Elsewhere, Paul urges wholehearted enthusiasm in all that one undertakes, but that does not mean the abuse of over-indulgence, greed, or coveting in the process (1 Cor. 10:31). One should not assume uncritically that there is in the Corinthian passage a proof text against all homosexuality or even all homosexual acts. Of course, homosexual behavior can be perverted and sinfully exploitative just as heterosexual activity can be—or any activity can be—but this is not the same as rejecting either sexual orientation or specific acts as sinful as such.[15]

On the surface this argument looks strong, but it is extremely weak when put to biblical and philosophical tests. It is true that an abuse argument in general is valid. Paul advocated temperance but not necessarily total abstinence. With regard to 1 Corinthians 6:9, it is correct that Christ-centered worship is the norm as opposed to the abuse of idolatry. It is also true that fornication and adultery are opposed to the norm of sexual relations under the sanctity of marriage. But to use the abuse argument, one must be consistent. In each instance the Bible clearly states the responsible norm as opposed to irresponsible or abusive behavior. A specific and consistent approach of this nature leads to a clear answer as to what is the responsible norm opposed to homosexuality. The responsible norm clearly taught in Scripture is heterosexuality in marriage. Gay theologians say that homosexual love is not mentioned or condemned in Scripture. They are correct in saying that homosexual love is nowhere mentioned in Scripture. The Bible refers only to lust and degrading passions, as in Romans 1.

Scripture never approves any form of sexual love within a homosexual relationship. The polarity that brings people together was created to function only between men and women. Each homosexual act in and of itself is the abuse. There is no such thing as nonabusive adultery; all adultery is wrong. There is no such thing as nonillicit theft; the Bible clearly states that all theft is wrong. Nor does the Bible teach such a thing as "responsible" covetousness. The Bible emphatically declares that all reviling and swindling is illicit. And without a doubt, homosexuality is placed in the same list of prohibitions in 1 Corinthians 6:9 and 1 Timothy 1:10. In the case of homosexuality, motives are not the issue. Homosexuality, according to the Bible, is wrong. It is an intrinsic evil.

In Romans 1:24-27 Paul discussed God's wrath over man's sin. It is a devastating passage for the practicing homosexual. But nevertheless it is used by gay theologians to affirm homosexual behavior. They say that the Romans passage discusses only a particular kind of homosexual activity and in no way condemns the sexual activity of the 20th-century person who is exclusively homosexual. It is impossible for a homosexual to "leave" the natural use of the opposite sex, because for him homosexuality is natural and heterosexuality is unnatural.

Note these key words: *change, leaving.* In order to change from or to leave heterosexuality, one must first be heterosexual. What we have is an account of bisexual lust—and St. Paul does say lust, placing this behavior out of the higher realm of love and devotion.

Two assumptions lie behind this type of reasoning: homosexuality is constitutional, and Paul was not aware of the different types of homosexuality that existed along with their causes. They say that what the Romans passage teaches is a disdain for hedonistic heterosexuals whose jaded appetites turn them from their own sexuality toward the unnatural state of homosexuality.

As far as Paul's knowledge of such sins is concerned, it must be remembered that Tarsus was the third-ranking intellectual city in the world, behind Athens and Alexandria. Paul grew up there and would have learned about the Greco-Roman world along with its assorted philosophies and practices. He could quote the Stoic poets. He had learned popular debating techniques. He could cite familiar Stoic virtues. In Tarsus he would have learned about the homosexual practice called pederasty. He would have been familiar with the view among certain Greeks that homosexuality was a highly regarded form of love. This is important to consider when analyzing Paul's inspired writings on this subject.

But there is also another explanation offered by gay theologians:

> In the letter [to the Romans] the practice is seen as a resultant and unfortunate structural problem in the world after the Fall from the original created order. Other of these evidences which Paul mentions are disobedience to parents, envy, and gossip. The homosexual reference, however, seems literarily most fitting since it illustrates what was perceived to be a reversal of a norm variously described by Paul as the exchange of the truth for a lie, professing wisdom for foolishness, and honoring and serving the creature more than the Creator.[16]

Blair is foggy here because he has a hard time explaining this passage away. It is destructive to his cause. The "unfortunate structural problem" is a euphemism for sin. This is why envy and gossip are included in the list. Gossip and envy are "unfortunate structural problems." The "reversal of a norm" is also another way of saying sin and depravity. Calling sin "soap" does not make it any less dirty in God's eyes. It does not make sense for Blair to say that homosexuality is just an illustration of depravity if homosexuality is not itself depraved. It is a self-defeating statement.

Paul gives a theological rationale for the mandatory condemnation of homosexual behavior. God's judgment gives persons freedom to go their own way. "God gave them up" to do what they wanted. The extent of divine judgment is emphasized by the threefold use of the Greek word for "gave up." "Wherefore God gave them up in lusts of their hearts to impurity, that their bodies might be dishonored among them. . . . For this reason God gave them up to degrading passions: for their women exchanged the natural function for the unnatural. . . . And just as they did not see fit to retain the full knowledge of God, God gave them up to a depraved mind, to do the things which are not proper" (Rom. 1:24, 26, 28, author's translation).

The statement "God gave them up" describes a judicial act.[17] God did more than withdraw His restraining force from mankind; He gave them over to judgment. Johnson elaborates on this point.

> The precisely identical form is in Acts 7:42 where, in speaking of Israel's apostasy in the days of Moses, Stephen says, "Then God turned, and gave them up to worship the host of heaven." Both the Romans and the Acts passages describe the act of God as a penal infliction of retribution, the expression of an essential attribute consistent with His holiness.[18]

Sexual rebellion is the retributive judgment of God. Romans 1:24-27 also looks back to the Genesis account.

> For example, the phrases "to birds and four-footed beasts, and creeping things" (v. 23) is surely reminiscent of "the fowl of the air, and over the cattle, and over all the earth" (Gen. 1:26; cf. vv. 20-25). And, further, the phrases "the glory of the uncorruptible God into an image

(lit., the likeness of an image) made like to corruptible man" appear to come from the Genesis account's "Let us make man in our image, after our likeness" (1:26).[19]

The fact that Paul's argument is tied inseparably to the Genesis account of divine judgment destroys the "abuse" argument and the constitutional assumption of homosexuality advocates. The act of homosexuality per se is wrong. It does not matter what the motives are. It does not matter about one's genetic makeup or hormone count. The act of homosexuality in and of itself is wrong. Paul spoke of individuals being consumed with passion for one another. That sounds definitely like someone with a homosexual orientation. When Paul wrote about women exchanging "natural relations" for unnatural (Rom. 1:27), he implied that they were exclusively homosexual in practice. They were confirmed, practicing homosexuals, not heterosexuals experimenting with homosexuality. Because of sin, normal sex drives are channeled into "against nature" expressions. There is no difference between what Paul described in Romans 1 and what the advocates of homosexuality today are trying to elevate to a respectable level.

Paul traced mankind's suffering, sorrow, and sin back to the sin of worshiping the creation rather than the Creator. This rebellion caused an impossible barrier in man's relationship to God. But the barrier did not quit there. That was just the root cause. The consequences continued. Barriers began to develop between persons. An individual's relationship to himself and to his fellowman was disturbed. Homosexuality is a glaring example of this broken personal identity. The confusion in man's relationships began with a break in his communion with God. Paul was saying that not only idolatry but also certain sexual practices changed the created order. A male is supposed to worship God, and in marriage he is to have sex with his wife. A female is supposed to worship God, and in marriage she is to have sex with her husband. When people defy God's order by worshiping creatures, they are judged with a further violation of the created order; they have intercourse

61

with members of the same sex.[20] Paul made no distinction between homosexual lust and behavior. He rejected homosexuality and categorically condemned it as sinful.

First Corinthians 6:9-10 and 1 Timothy 1:10, discussed earlier, condemn male homosexuality. Only wild speculation can avoid the conclusion that Paul knew exactly what he meant and how he should be understood when he spoke against these sinful practices.

CONCLUSION

Believers are to love homosexuals, but one must be suspicious of any position that approaches Scripture with a condescending mentality. If the Bible disagrees with their position, then gay theologians will try to win their argument with an emotional approach under the guise of love. To them, the real issue is not the Scriptures, but acceptance.

> The Bible is man's source to understanding Christ. But believers need to spend more time observing His spirit as related there rather than the "letter of the law" given by His followers in attempting to spread His message. Pick up an edition of the Bible with Christ's recorded statements printed in red. Study only His words, comparing His positive approach throughout the Scriptures. Notice His emphasis on love—His silence on the means of sex but concern only with the motives behind it.[21]

Granted, Christ had a "love morality"; but it was combined with and defined by a "law morality." "Whosoever therefore shall break one of the least of these commandments, and shall teach men to do so, he shall be called the least in the kingdom of heaven: but whosoever shall do and teach them, the same shall be called great in the kingdom of heaven" (Matt. 5:19). For Christ there was no conflict between law and love. He spoke of love fulfilling the law.

Pro-homosexuality writers warp the Scriptures. They are more interested in the feelings of sinners than in the clear guidelines of God's Word. They are more concerned with making homosexuals feel accepted than they are in pointing them to the Savior. Love is "that which seeks the will of God in the object loved."[22] Homosexuality is not the will of God. Homosexual behavior can never be "the loving thing to do."

NOTES

1. D. Sherwin Bailey, *Homosexuality and the Western Christian Tradition* (London: Longmans, Green & Co., 1955; reprint, Hamden, Conn.: Shoestring Press, 1975).
2. John Boswell, *Christianity, Social Tolerance, and Homosexuality* (Chicago: University of Chicago Press, 1980).
3. Bailey, *Homosexuality*, 5.
4. Ibid., 4.
5. Ibid., 3–5.
6. Derek Kidner, *Genesis: An Introduction and Commentary*, Tyndale Old Testament Commentaries (Chicago: InterVarsity Press, 1963), 137.
7. Richard Wolff, *A Commentary on the Epistle of Jude* (Grand Rapids: Zondervan Publishing House, 1960), 75.
8. Josephus, quoted in Wolff, *Jude*, 76–77.
9. Boswell, *Christianity, Social Tolerance, and Homosexuality*, 95.
10. Ralph Blair, *An Evangelical Look at Homosexuality* (Chicago: Moody Press, 1963), 3.
11. Letha Scanzoni and Virginia Ramey Mollenkott, *Is the Homosexual My Neighbor?* (San Francisco: Harper & Row, 1978), 60–61.
12. Blair, *An Evangelical Look at Homosexuality*, 3.
13. Charles C. Ryrie, *The Grace of God* (Chicago: Moody Press, 1963), 105–13.
14. Charles C. Ryrie, "The End of the Law," *Bibliotheca Sacra* 124 (July–September 1967): 246.
15. Ralph Blair, *An Evangelical Look at Homosexuality* (Chicago: Moody Press, 1963), 6.
16. Blair, *An Evangelical Look at Homosexuality*, 7.
17. S. Lewis Johnson, Jr., "God Gave Them Up," *Bibliotheca Sacra* 129 (April–June 1972): 127–28.

18. Ibid., 128.
19. Ibid., 132.
20. David L. Bartlett, "Biblical Perspective on Homosexuality," *Foundations: Baptist Journal of History and Theology* 20 (April–June 1977): 140.
21. Kim Stablinski, "Homosexuality: What the Bible Does and Does Not Say," *The Ladder,* July 1969, n.p.
22. Charles Ryrie, *A Survey of Bible Doctrine* (Chicago: Moody Press, 1972), 21.

5
PORNOGRAPHY
J. Kerby Anderson

Pornography is tearing apart the very fabric of our society. Yet Christians are often ignorant of its impact and apathetic about the need to control this menace.

It is an $8-billion-a-year business with close ties to organized crime.[1] Purveyors of pornography reap enormous profits through sales in so-called "adult bookstores" and viewing of films and live acts at theaters.

To some, pornography is nothing more than a few pictures of scantily-clad women in seductive poses. But it has become much more. Pornography involves books, magazines, videos, and devices and has moved from the periphery of society into the mainstream through the renting of videocassettes, sales of so-called "soft-porn" magazines, and the airing of sexually explicit movies on cable television.

THE FACTS OF PORNOGRAPHY

Nearly 900 theaters show X-rated films and more than 15,000 "adult" bookstores and video stores offer pornographic material. Adult bookstores outnumber McDonald's restaurants in the U.S.[2] Each year nearly 100 pornographic films are distributed to "adult" theaters providing estimated annual box office sales of $50 million.

Definitions

The 1986 Attorney General Commission on Pornography defined pornography as material that "is predominantly sexually explicit and intended primarily for the purpose of sexual arousal." Hard-core pornography "is sexually explicit in the extreme, and devoid of any other apparent content or purpose."[3]

Another important term is the definition of obscenity. The current legal definition of obscenity is found in the 1973 case of *Miller vs. California.* According to the *Miller* case, material is obscene if all three of the following conditions are met:

(1) The average person, applying contemporary community standards, would find that the work, taken as a whole, appeals to the prurient interests.

(2) The work depicts or describes, in a patently offensive way, sexual conduct specifically defined by the applicable state (or federal) law, and

(3) The work, taken as a whole, lacks serious, artistic, political or scientific value.[4]

Types of Pornography

The first type of pornography is adult magazines. These are primarily directed toward an adult male audience (but not exclusively). The magazines which have the widest distribution (e.g., *Playboy, Penthouse)* do not violate the *Miller* standard of obscenity and thus can be legally distributed. But other magazines which do violate these standards are still readily available in many adult bookstores.

The second type of pornography is videocassettes. These are rented or sold in most adult bookstores and have become a growth industry for pornography. People who would not go into an adult bookstore or theater to watch a pornographic movie will obtain these videocassettes through bookstores or the mail and watch them in the privacy of their homes. Usually these videos display a high degree of hard-core pornography. The third type of pornography is motion pictures. Rating standards are being relaxed, and many pornographic movies are being shown and distributed carrying R and X ratings. Many of these so-called "hard R" rated films would have been considered obscene just a decade ago.

A fourth type of pornography is television. As in motion pictures, standards for commercial television have been continuously lowered. But an even greater threat is on cable television. The Federal Communications Commission does not regulate cable in the same way it does public access stations. Thus many pornographic movies are shown on cable television. Like videocassettes, cable TV provides the average person with easy access to pornographic material. People who would never go to an adult bookstore can now view the same sexually explicit material in the privacy of their homes, making cable TV "the ultimate brown wrapper."

A fifth type of pornography is audio porn. This includes "Dial-a-porn" telephone calls, which are the second fastest growth market of pornography. Though most of the messages are within the *Miller* definition of obscenity, these businesses continue to thrive and are often used by children.

While serving on the Attorney General's Commission on Pornography, Dr. James Dobson discovered how vile pornography could be. The following is his graphic description of the pornography trade in America:

> X-rated movies and magazines feature oral, anal, and genital sex between women and donkeys, pigs, horses, dogs, and dozens of other animals. In a single sex shop in New York City, there were 46 films and videos available which featured bestiality of every type. Other offerings focused on so-called "bathroom sports" including urination (golden showers), defecation, eating feces and spreading them on the face and body, mutilation of every type (including voluntary amputation, fishhooks through genetalia, fists in rectums, mousetraps on breasts), oral

and anal sex between groups of men and women, and (forgive me) the drinking of ejaculate in champagne glasses. Simulated child pornography depicts females who are actually 18 years of age or older but appear to be 14 or 15. They are shown with shaved genitalia, with ribbons in their hair and surrounded by teddy bears. Their "fathers" are often pictured with them in consummate incestuous settings. The magazines in sex shops are organized on shelves according to topic, such as Gay Violence, Vomiting, Rape, Enemas, and topics that I cannot describe even in a frank discussion of this nature.[5]

According to Henry Boatwright, chairman of the U.S. Advisory Board for Social Concerns, approximately 70 percent of the pornographic magazines sold end up in the hands of minors. Women Against Pornography estimate that about 1.2 million children are annually exploited in commercial sex (child pornography and prostitution).

According to Charles Keating of Citizens for Decency Through Law, research reveals that 77 percent of child molesters of boys and 87 percent of child molesters of girls admitted imitating the sexual behavior they had seen modeled in pornography.

THE DOCUMENTED EFFECTS OF PORNOGRAPHY

However, defenders of pornography argue that it is not harmful, and thus should not be regulated or banned. In 1970 the Presidential Commission on Obscenity and Pornography concluded there was no relationship between exposure to erotic material and subsequent behavior. But more than a decade of research, as well as the production of more explicit and violent forms of pornography, have shown that pornography can have profound effects on human behavior.

The 1986 Attorney General's Commission on Pornography examined the effects of five different classes of material: (1)

sexually violent material, (2) nonviolent materials depicting degradation, domination, subordination, or humiliation, (3) nonviolent and nondegrading materials, (4) nudity, and (5) child pornography. The first two categories demonstrated negative effects, the third showed mixed results, the fourth was not found harmful but Commissioners agreed it was morally objectionable, and the fifth involves sexual exploitation and is already outlawed.

Psychological Effects

Psychologist Edward Donnerstein of the University of Wisconsin found that brief exposure to violent forms of pornography can lead to anti-social attitudes and behavior. Male viewers tend to be more aggressive toward women, less responsive to pain and suffering of rape victims, and more willing to accept various myths about rape.[6]

Dr. Dolf Zillman and Dr. Jennings Bryant showed that continued exposure to pornography had serious adverse effects on beliefs about sexuality in general and on attitudes toward women in particular. They also found that pornography desensitizes people to rape as a criminal offense.[7] These researchers also found that massive exposure to pornography encourages a desire for increasingly deviant materials which involve violence, including sadomasochism and rape.[8]

Feminist author Diana Russell notes the correlation between deviant behavior (including abuse) and pornography. She also found that pornography leads men and women to experience conflict, suffering, and sexual dissatisfaction.[9] Statistical studies by sociologists Larry Baron and Murray Straus of the University of New Hampshire found that rape rates are highest in states that have high sales of sex magazines and lax enforcement of pornography laws.[10]

Michigan state police detective Darrell Pope found that in 41 percent of the 38,000 sexual assault cases in Michigan between 1956 and 1979, pornographic material was viewed by the offenders just before or during the crime. This corroborates with research done by psychotherapist David Scott who found that "half the rapists studied used pornography to arouse themselves immediately prior to seeking out a victim."[11]

Addiction to Pornography

Researcher Victor Cline of the University of Utah has documented how men become addicted to pornographic materials, begin to desire more explicit or deviant material, and end up acting out what they have seen.[12]

Psychologists have identified a five-step pattern in pornographic addiction.[13] The first step is exposure. Addicts have been exposed to pornography in many ways, ranging from sexual abuse as children to looking at widely available pornographic magazines.

The second step is addiction. People who continually expose themselves to pornography "keep coming back for more and more" in order to get new sexual highs. Dr. James L. McCough, of the University of California at Irvine, says that "Experiences at times of emotional or sexual arousal get locked in the brain by the chemical epinephrine and become virtually impossible to erase."[14]

A third step is escalation. Previous sexual highs become more difficult to attain. Therefore people begin to look for more exotic forms of sexual behavior to bring them stimulation.

A fourth step is desensitization. What was initially shocking becomes routine. Shocking and disgusting sexual behavior is no longer avoided but sought out for more intense stimulation. Concern about pain gets lost in the pursuit of the next sexual experience.

A fifth step is acting out the fantasies. People do what they have seen and find pleasurable. Not every pornography addict will become a serial murderer or a rapist. But many do look for ways to act out their sexual fantasies.

The Final Report of the 1986 Attorney General's Commission on Pornography lists a full chapter of testimony from victims whose assailants had previously viewed pornographic materials. The adverse effects range from physical harm (rape, torture, murder, sexually transmitted diseases) to psychological harm (suicidal thoughts, fear, shame, nightmares).

Social Effects

A frequent argument from civil libertarians and defenders of pornography is that it does not have any social effects. In fact, some argue that pornography can have a therapeutic effect on society.

One of the frequently cited studies by pornographers is a study done by Kutchinsky in the Netherlands which alleged that the number of reported sex crimes dropped after legalization. His theory was that the availability of pornography siphons off dangerous sex impulses. But when the data for his "safety valve" theory was further evaluated, it was found that he lumped together voyeurism and homosexuality (which police stopped reporting after legalization) with rapes (which actually increased in number).[15]

Deborah Baker, a legal assistant and executive director of DCAD, an anti-obscenity group, explains the difficulty of scientifically demonstrating a connection between pornography and crime:

The argument that there are no established studies showing a connection between pornography and violent crime is merely a smokescreen. Those who promote this stance well know that such research will never be done. It would require a sampling of much more than a thousand males, exposed to pornography through puberty and adolescence, while the other group is totaly isolated from its influence in all its forms and varying degrees. Each group would then have to be monitored — through the commission of violent crimes or not. In spite of the lack of formal research, though, the FBI's own statistics show that pornography is found at 80 percent of the scenes of

71

violent sex crimes, or in the homes of the perpetrators.[16]

Nevertheless, there are a number of compelling statistics that suggest that pornography does have profound social consequences. For example, of the 1,400 child sexual molestation cases in Louisville, Kentucky, between July 1980 and February 1984, adult pornography was connected with each incident and child pornography with the majority of them.[17] Police officers have seen the impact pornography has had on serial murderers. In fact, pornography consumption is one of the most common profile characteristics of serial murderers and rapists.[18]

In his introduction to a reprint of the Final Report of the Attorney General's Commission on Pornography, columnist Michael McManus noted the following:

> The FBI interviewed two dozen sex murderers in prison who had killed multiple numbers of times. Some eighty-one percent said their biggest sexual interest was in reading pornography. They acted out sex fantasies on real people. For example, Arthur Gary Bishop, convicted of sexually abusing and killing five young boys, said, "If pornographic material would have been unavailable to me in my early states, it is most probable that my sexual activities would not have escalated to the degree they did." He said pornography's impact on him was "devastating. . . I am a homosexual pedophile convicted of murder, and pornography was a determing factor in my downfall."[19]

Dr. James Dobson interviewed Ted Bundy, one of this nation's most notorious serial killers. On the day before his execution, Ted Bundy said that the "most damaging kinds of pornography are those that involve violence and sexual violence. Because the wedding of those two forces, as I know only too well, brings about behavior that is just, just too terrible to describe."[20]

CENSORSHIP AND FREEDOM OF SPEECH

Attempts to regulate and outlaw pornography within a community are frequently criticized as censorship and a violation of the First Amendment rights of the producer and viewer. But the Supreme Court clearly stated in *Roth vs. United States* (1957) that obscenity was not protected by the First Amendment. Federal, state, and local laws apply to the sale, display, distribution, and broadcast of pornography. Pornographic material therefore can be prohibited if it meets the legal definition of obscenity.

The Supreme Court ruled in the case of *Miller vs. California* (1973) that a legal definition of obscenity must meet the three-part test discussed earlier in this chapter. If it appeals to the prurient interest, is patently offensive, and lacks serious value (artistically, etc.), then the material is considered obscene and is illegal.

The Supreme Court further ruled in *Paris Adult Theatre vs. Slaton* (1973) that material legally defined as obscene is not accorded the same protection as free speech in the First Amendment. The court ruled that even if obscene films are shown only to "consenting adults," this did not grant them immunity from the law.

In the case of *New York vs. Ferber* (1982) the Supreme Court ruled that child pornography was not protected under the First Amendment even if it was not legally defined as obscene under their three-part test. Since children cannot legally consent to sexual relations, child pornography constitutes sexual abuse. Congress also passed the Child Protection Act in 1984 which provided tougher restrictions on child pornography.

Cable television is presently unregulated since it is not technically "broadcasting" as defined in the Federal Communications Commission Act. Thus cable television is able to show pornographic movies with virtual impunity. The FCC Act needs to be amended so that the FCC can regulate cable television.

73

A BIBLICAL PERSPECTIVE

God created men and women in His image (Gen. 1:27) as sexual beings. But because of sin in the world (Rom. 3:23), sex has been misused and abused (Rom. 1:24-25).

Pornography attacks the dignity of men and women created in the image of God. Pornography also distorts God's gift of sex which should be shared only within the bonds of marriage (1 Cor. 7:2-3).

A biblical perspective of human sexuality must recognize that sexual intercourse is exclusively reserved for marriage for the following purposes. First, it establishes the one-flesh union (Gen. 2:24-25, Matt. 19:4-6). Second, it provides for sexual intimacy within the marriage bond. The use of the word *know* indicates sexual intercourse (Gen. 4:1). Third, sexual inter-course is for the mutual pleasure of husband and wife (Prov. 5:18-19). Fourth, sexual intercourse provides for procreation (Gen. 1:28).

The Bible warns against the misuse of sex. Premarital and extramarital sex is condemned (1 Cor. 6:13-18, 1 Thes. 4:3). Even thoughts of sexual immorality (often fed by pornographic material) are condemned (Matt. 5:27-28).

Scripture specifically condemns the practices that result from pornography such as sexual exposure (Gen. 9:21-23; Ex. 20:26), adultery (Lev. 18:20), bestiality (Lev. 18:23), homo-sexuality (Lev. 18:22, 20:13), incest (Lev. 18:6-18), and pros-titution (Deut. 23:17-18).

Christians must realize that pornography can have significant harmful effects on the user. These include a comparison men-tality, a performance-based sexuality, a feeling that only for-bidden things are sexually satisfying, increased guilt, de-creased self-concept, and obsessional thinking.[21]

Christians therefore must do two things. First, they must keep themselves pure by fleeing immorality (1 Cor. 6:18) and thinking on those things that are pure (Phil. 4:8). "As a man thinks in his heart, so is he." Christians must "not think about how to gratify the desires of the sinful nature" (Rom. 13:14).

74

Pornography will fuel the sexual desire in abnormal ways and can eventually lead to even more debase perversion. We therefore must "abstain from sinful desires, which war against your soul" (1 Peter 2:11). Second, Christians must work to remove this sexual perversion of pornography from society.

POSITIVE STEPS TO COMBAT PORN

One of the first steps in combatting porn is parents teaching a wholesome, biblical view of sex to their children. Helpful aids can be obtained from groups like Focus on the Family and Josh McDowell Ministries.

Second, we must evaluate our exposure to media (magazines, TV shows, music) with inappropriate sexual themes. Parents should set a positive example for their children, and take time to discuss these stories, programs, and songs with them.

Third, pastors should warn their congregations about the dangers of pornography and instruct them in a proper view of sexuality. Like Joseph in the Old Testament, we should flee immorality. Help should also be given to build strong Christian homes.

Fourth, Christians should get involved with local decency groups organized to fight pornography. These groups have been effective in ridding many communities of the pornography plague.

Fifth, Christians should express concern to local officials (through letters and petitions) about X-rated movie houses and adult bookstores in their communities.

Sixth, if a person receives pornographic material in the mail, he should report it to his postmaster and request that federal agents take action.

Seventh, Christians should not patronize stores that sell pornographic materials. Organizing a boycott and picketing can help get community attention focused on the problem.

Sixth, believers should encourage their federal and state

representatives to implement the recommendations from the Attorney General's Commission on Pornography and use existing legislation to prosecute those who distribute obscenity.

NOTES

1. William Stanmeyer, *The Seduction of Society* (Ann Arbor, Mich.: Servant Books, 1984), 39–48.
2. Tom Minnery, ed., *Pornography: A Human Tragedy* (Wheaton, Ill.: Living Books, 1987), 43.
3. *Final Report of the Attorney General's Commission on Pornography,* ed. Michael McManus (Nashville, Tenn.: Rutledge Hill Press, 1986), 8.
4. Ibid., 17–18.
5. Minnery, *Pornography: A Human Tragedy,* 35.
6. Edward Donnerstein, "Pornography and Violence Against Women, *Annal of the New York Academy of Science* 347(1980), 277–288.
7. Dolf Zillman and Jennings Bryant, "Pornography, Sexual Callousness, and the Trivialization of Rape," *Journal of Communication* 32 (1982), 10–21.
8. Zillman, Bryant, Carveth, "The Effect of Erotica Featuring Sadomasochism and Beastiality on Motivated Inter-Male Aggression," *Personality and Social Psychology Bulletin* 7 (1981), 153–159.
9. Diana Russell, *Rape and Marriage,* 1982.
10. Larry Baron and Murray Straus, "Legitimate Violence and Rape: A Test of the Cultural Spillover Theory," *Social Problems* 34 (December 1985).
11. David Alexander Scott, "How Pornography Changes Attitudes," in *Pornography: A Human Tragedy.*
12. Victor Cline, *Where Do You Draw the Line?* (Provo, Utah: Brigham Young University Press, 1974).
13. Modified from "The Power of Porn," by Kenneth Kantzer, in *Christianity Today* 7 February 1986, 18.
14. Ibid.
15. *Final Report,* ed. McManus, 259–60.
16. Deborah Baker, "Pornography Isn't Free Speech," *Dallas Morning News* 17 March 1989, op. ed. page.
17. Testimony by John B. Rabun, deputy director, National Center for Missing and Exploited Children, before the Subcommittee on Juvenile Justice of the United States Senate Judiciary Committee, September 12, 1984.

18. *The Men Who Murdered,* FBI Law Enforcement Bulletin, August 1985.
19. *Final Report,* ed. McManus, p. xvii.
20. Interview by Dr. James Dobson with Ted Bundy in Starke, Florida on January 23, 1989.
21. Earl D. Wilson, *Sexual Sanity: Breaking Free from Uncontrolled Habits* (Downers Grove, Ill.: InterVarsity Press, 1984), 72–82.

6
DRUG ABUSE
J. Kerby Anderson

n the 1960s, the drug culture became a part of American society. What was once the pastime of Timothy Leary's disciples and the habit of poverty-stricken junkies went mainline to the middle class. A culture that once lived in the safe world of Ozzie and Harriet awoke to the stark realization that even their son Ricky used cocaine.

The statistics are staggering. The average age of first alcohol use is 12 and the average age of first drug use is 13. According to the National Institute on Drug Abuse, 93 percent of all teenagers have some experience with alcohol by the end of their senior year of high school, and 6 percent drink daily. Almost two-thirds of all American young people try illicit drugs before they finish high school. One out of 16 seniors smokes marijuana daily, and 20 percent have done so for at least a month sometime in their lives.[1]

But Americans have changed their minds about drugs. A Gallup poll released on the twentieth anniversary of Woodstock showed that drugs, once an integral part of the counter-culture, are considered to be the number-one problem in America. Two decades before, young people tied drugs to their "search for peace, love, and good times." But by 1989, Americans associated drugs "with danger, crime and despair."[2]

A similar conclusion can be found among the nation's teenagers. A Gallup poll of 500 teens found that 60 percent said

78

concern over drug abuse was their greatest fear — outranking fear of AIDS, alcohol, unemployment, and war.[3]

Nationwide surveys indicate that about 90 percent of the nation's youth experiment with alcohol—currently teenagers' drug of choice. An annual survey conducted by the University of Michigan has revealed the extent to which young people drink. Over 65 percent of the nation's seniors currently drink. And about 40 percent reported a heavy drinking episode within the two weeks prior to the survey.[4]

Another survey released by the University of Colorado shows that the problem of drug use is not just outside the church. The study involved nearly 14,000 junior high and high school youth. It compared churched young people with unchurched young people and found very little difference.

For example, 88 percent of the unchurched young people reported drinking beer, as compared to 80 percent of churched young people. When asked how many had tried marijuana, 47 percent of the unchurched young people had done so, compared to 38 percent of the churched youth. For amphetamines and barbiturates, 28 percent of the unchurched had tried them, while 22 percent of the churched young people had tried them. And for cocaine use, the percentage was 14 percent for unchurched youths and 11 percent for churched youths.[5]

TYPES OF DRUGS

Alcohol

Alcohol is the most common drug used and abused. It is an intoxicant which depresses the central nervous system and can bring a temporary loss of control over physical and mental powers. The signs of drunkenness are well known: lack of coordination, slurred speech, blurred vision, and poor judgment.

The amount of alcohol is measured by a "proof rating." For example, 45 percent pure alcohol would be 90 proof liquor. A

12-ounce can of beer, 4 ounces of wine, and 1 shot glass of 100 proof liquor all contain the same amount of alcohol.

In recent years, debate has raged over whether alcoholism is a sin or a sickness.[6] The Bible clearly labels drunkenness a sin (Deut. 21:20-21; 1 Cor. 6:9-10; Gal. 5:19-20), but that does not mitigate against the growing physiological evidence that certain people's biochemistry make them more prone to addiction.

Some studies suggest that the body chemistry of alcoholics processes alcohol differently than non-alcoholics. Acetaldehyde is the intermediate by-product of alcohol metabolism. But the biochemistry of some people make it difficult to process acetaldehyde into acetate. Thus, acetaldehyde builds up in the body and begins to affect a person's brain chemistry. The chemicals produced (called isoquinolines) act very much like opiates and therefore contribute to alcoholism.[7]

Other studies have revealed a connection between certain kinds of personalities and alcoholism. The general conclusion has been that there is no connection.[8] But more recent studies seem to suggest some correlation between personality type and drug abuse. One personality type that seems to be at risk is the anti-social personality (ASP) who is often charming, manipulative, impulsive, and egocentric. He makes up 25 percent of the alcohol and drug abuse population, yet comprises only about 3 percent of the general population.[9]

The social costs of alcohol are staggering. Alcoholism is the third largest health problem (following heart disease and cancer). There are an estimated 10 million problem drinkers in the American adult population and an estimated 3.3 million teenage problem drinkers. Half of all traffic fatalities and one-third of all traffic injuries are alcohol-related. Alcohol is involved in 67 percent of all murders and 33 percent of all suicides.[10]

Alcohol is also a prime reason for the breakdown of the family. A high percentage of family violence, parental abuse and neglect, lost wages, and divorce is tied to the abuse of alcohol in this country. In one poll on alcohol done for *Chris-*

Family Today by George Gallup, nearly one fourth of all Americans cited alcohol and/or drug abuse as one of the three reasons most responsible for the high divorce rate in this country.[11]

Since the publication of Janet Geringer Woititz's book *Adult Children of Alcoholics,* society has begun to understand the long-term effect of alcoholism on future generations. Children of alcoholics (COAs) exhibit a number of traits including guessing what normal behavior is, having difficulty following a project from beginning to end, judging themselves without mercy, and having difficulty with intimate relationships.[12]

The toxic effects of alcohol are also well known. Alcohol often causes permanent damage to vital organs such as the brain and the liver. Death occurs if alcohol is taken in large enough amounts. When the blood alcohol level reaches 40/100s of 1%, unconsciousness occurs, and at 50/100s of 1%, alcoholic poisoning and death occurs.[13]

Marijuana

Marijuana is produced from the hemp plant *(Cannabis sativa)* that grows well throughout the world. Marijuana has been considered a "gateway drug" because of its potential to lead young people to experiment with stronger drugs such as heroin and cocaine. By 1978, an alarming 10 percent of all high school seniors smoked marijuana every day. Though that percentage has dropped significantly, officials still estimate that about one-third of all teenagers have tried marijuana.[14]

Marijuana is an intoxicant which is usually smoked in order to induce a feeling of euphoria that lasts two to four hours. Several observed physical effects include increased heart rate, bloodshot eyes, a dry mouth and throat, and increased appetite. Marijuana can impair or reduce short-term memory and comprehension. It can reduce one's ability to perform tasks requiring concentration (such as driving a car). Marijuana can also produce paranoia and psychosis.

Because most marijuana users inhale unfiltered smoke and

hold it in their lungs for as long as possible, it causes damage to the lungs and pulmonary system. Marijuana smoke has more cancer-causing agents than tobacco smoke. Marijuana also interferes with the immune system and reduces sperm count in males.

Cocaine

Cocaine occurs naturally in the leaves of coca plants and was reportedly chewed by natives in Peru as early as the 6th century. It became widely used in beverages (like Coca-Cola) and medicines in the 19th century, but was restricted in 1914 by the Harrison Narcotics Act.

Some experts estimate that more than 30 million Americans have tried cocaine. Government surveys suggest there may be as many as 6 million regular users.[15] Every day some 5,000 persons sniff a line of coke for the first time.[16] Today the government estimates that more than 300,000 Americans are intravenous cocaine abusers.[17]

In recent years, snorting cocaine has given way to smoking it. Snorting cocaine limits the intensity of the effect because the blood vessels in the nose are constricted. Smoking cocaine delivers a much more intense high. A smoke goes directly to the lungs and then to the heart. On the next heartbeat, it is on the way to the brain.

Dr. Anna Rose Childress, at the University of Pennsylvania, notes that "you can become compulsively involved with snorted cocaine. We have many Hollywood movie stars without nasal septums to prove that." But when cocaine is smoked "it seems to have incredibly powerful effects that tend to set up a compulsive addictive cycle more quickly than anything that we've seen."[18]

Until recently, people speaking of cocaine dependence would never call it an addiction. Cocaine's withdrawal symptoms are not physically wrenching like those of heroin and alcohol. Yet cocaine involves compulsion, loss of control, and continued use in spite of the consequences.

Cocaine is a stimulant and increases heart rate, restricts blood vessels, and stimulates mental awareness. Users say it is an ego builder. Along with increased energy comes a feeling of personal supremacy: the illusion of being smarter, sexier, more competent than anyone else. But while the cocaine confidence makes users feel indestructible, the crash from cocaine leaves them depressed, paranoid, and searching for more.

The death of University of Maryland basketball star Len Bias and an article by Dr. Jeffrey Isner in the *New England Journal of Medicine* that same year have established that cocaine can cause fatal heart problems. These deaths can occur regardless of whether the user has had previous heart problems and regardless of how the cocaine was taken.[19]

Cocaine users also describe its effect in sexual terms. Its intense and sensual effect make it a stronger aphrodisiac than sex itself. Research at UCLA with apes given large amounts of cocaine showed they preferred the drug to food or sexual partners and were willing to endure severe electric shocks in exchange for large doses.[20]

The cocaine problem in this country has been made worse by the introduction of crack. Ordinary coke is mixed with baking soda and water into a solution and heated. This material is then dried and broken into tiny chunks that resemble rock candy. Users usually smoke these crack rocks in glass pipes. Crack (so called because of the cracking sound it makes when heated) has become the scourge from the drug business. A single hit of crack provides an intense, wrenching rush in a matter of seconds. Because crack is absorbed rapidly through the lungs and hits the brain within seconds, it is the most dangerous form of cocaine and also the most addicting.

Another major difference between crack and ordinary cocaine is the cost. According to Dr. Mark Gold, founder of the nationwide cocaine hotline, the cost to an addict using crack is one-tenth the cost he would have paid for the equivalent in cocaine powder just a decade ago.[21] Since crack costs much less than normal cocaine, it is particularly appealing to adolescents. About one in five 12th-graders has tried cocaine, and that percentage is certain to increase because of the price and availability of crack.

Hallucinogens

The hallucinogenic drug of choice during the 1960s was LSD. People looking for the "ultimate trip" would take LSD or perhaps peyote and experience bizarre illusions and hallucinations.

In the last few decades, these hallucinogens have been replaced by PCP (phencyclidine), often known as "angel dust" or "killer weed." First synthesized in the 1950s as an anesthetic, PCP was discontinued because of its side effects but is now manufactured illegally and sold to thousands of teenagers.

PCP is often sprayed on cigarettes or marijuana and then smoked. Users report a sense of distance and estrangement. PCP creates body image distortion, dizziness, and double vision. The drug distorts reality in such a way that it can resemble mental illness. Because the drug blocks pain receptors, violent PCP episodes may result in self-inflicted injuries.

Chronic PCP users have persistent memory problems and speech difficulties. Mood disorders, such as depression, anxiety, and violent behavior, are also reported. High doses of PCP can produce a coma which can last for days or weeks.

Synthetic Drugs

The latest scourges from the drug business are the so-called "designer drugs." These synthetic drugs manufactured in underground laboratories mimic the effects of commonly abused drugs. Since they were not even anticipated when our current drug laws were written, they exist in a legal limbo, and the percentage of their use is increasing.

One drug is MDMA and is also known as "ecstasy." It has been called the "LSD of the 80s" and gives the user a cocaine-like rush with a hallucinogenic euphoria. Ecstasy was sold legally for a few years despite National Institute on Drug Abuse fears that it could cause brain damage. In 1985, the DEA outlawed MDMA, though it is still widely available.[22]

Other drugs have been marketed as a variation of the pain-killers Demerol and Fentanyl. The synthetic variation of the anesthetic Fentanyl is considered more potent than heroin and is known on the street as "synthetic heroin" or "China White."

Designer drugs may become a growth industry in the 90s. Creative drug makers in clandestine laboratories can produce these drugs for a fraction of the cost of smuggled drugs and with much less hassle from law enforcement.

BIBLICAL ANALYSIS

Some people may believe that the Bible has little to say about drugs, but this is not so. First, the Bible says much about the most common and most abused drug — that is, alcohol. Scripture admonishes Christians not to be drunk with wine (Eph. 5:18) and calls drunkenness a sin (Deut. 21:20-21; 1 Cor. 6:9-10; Gal. 5:19-20). The Bible also warns of the dangers of the abuse of alcohol (Prov. 20:1; Isa. 5:11; Hab. 2:15-16), and by implication, the danger of taking other kinds of drugs.

Second, drugs were an integral part of many ancient Near East societies. For example, the pagan cultures surrounding the nation of Israel used drugs as part of their religious cere-monies.[23] Both the Old Testament and New Testament con-demn sorcery and witchcraft. The word translated "sorcery" comes from the Greek word from which we get the English words *pharmacy* and *pharmaceutical*.[24] In ancient times, drugs were prepared by a witch or shaman. Drugs were used to enter into the spiritual world by inducing an altered state of consciousness that allowed demons to take over the mind of the user. In that day, drug use was tied to sorcery. In our day, many use drugs merely for so-called "recreational" purposes, but we cannot discount the occult connection.

Galatians 5:19-21 says: "The acts of the sinful nature are obvious: sexual immorality, impurity and debauchery; idolatry and witchcraft [which includes the use of drugs]; hatred, discord, jealousy, fits of rage, selfish ambition, dissensions, factions, and envy; drunkenness, orgies, and the like. I warn you, as I did before, that those who live like this will not inherit the kingdom of God."

The word *witchcraft* here is also translated "sorcery" and refers to the use of drugs. The Apostle Paul calls witchcraft that was associated with drug use a sin. The nonmedical use of drugs is considered one of the acts of a sinful nature. Using drugs, whether to "get a high" or to tap into the occult, is one of the acts of a sinful nature in which users demonstrate their depraved and carnal nature.

The psychic effects of drugs should not be discounted. A questionnaire designed by Charles Tate and sent to users of marijuana documented some disturbing findings. In his article in *Psychology Today* he noted that one-fourth of the marijuana users who responded to his questionnaire reported that they were taken over and controlled by an evil person or power during their drug-induced experience. And over half of those questioned said they have experienced religious or "spiritual" sensations in which they meet spiritual beings.[25]

Many proponents of the drug culture have linked drug use to spiritual values. During the 1960s, Timothy Leary and Alan Watts refered to the "religious" and "mystical" experience gained through the use of LSD (along with other drugs) as a prime reason for taking drugs.[26]

HOW PARENTS CAN KEEP THEIR CHILDREN OFF DRUGS

Drugs pose a threat to our children, but parents can protect them from much of this threat by working on the following preventive measures.

An important first step in keeping children off drugs is to build up their self-esteem. Children with a positive self image stand a better chance against peer pressure. Parents must help their children know they are a special creation of God (Ps. 139:13-16) and worthy of dignity and respect (Ps. 8:5-8).

Parents must help them see the fallacy of trying to conform to some group's standards by going along with its drug habits. Kids often think drugs are chic and cool. Parents must show their children that drugs are dangerous and work to counter the cliches of kids who will tempt their children to use drugs.

Second, parents should monitor their children's friendships. Before they allow their children to spend too much time with another child, parents should get to know the other child's family. Does the child come home to an empty house after school? Is there adult supervision of the children's activities? Often an unsupervised home invites drug experimentation.

A third thing parents can do is to promote alternatives to drugs. Schools and church groups should develop "Just Say No" clubs and programs. Parents should provide alternative activities for their children. Sports, school clubs, the arts, hobbies are all positive alternatives to the negative influence of drugs. At home, children should be encouraged to read books, play on a computer, or be involved in other activities that use the mind.

Fourth, parents should teach their children about drugs. Drug education can't just be left to the schools. Parents have to be personally involved and let their kids know that drugs won't be tolerated. Parents themselves should also be educated about drugs and drug paraphernalia.

Fifth, parents must set a good example. Parents who are drug-free have a much better chance of rearing drug-free children. If parents are using drugs, they should stop immediately. The unconditional message to our kids must be that drugs are wrong and they won't be tolerated in the home.

HOW PARENTS CAN RECOGNIZE DRUG ABUSE

Most parents simply do not believe their child could abuse drugs. But statistics suggest otherwise. Each year thousands of young people get hooked on drugs and alcohol. Parents must learn to recognize the symptoms of drug abuse.

The organization Straight, Inc. has produced the following checklist of eighteen warning signs of alcohol or drug abuse.[27]
1. School tardiness, truancy, declining grades
2. Less motivation, energy, self-discipline
3. Loss of interest in activities
4. Forgetfulness, short- or long-term
5. Short attention span, trouble concentrating
6. Aggressive anger, hostility, irritability
7. Sullen, uncaring attitudes and behavior
8. Family arguments, strife with family members
9. Disappearance of money, valuables
10. Changes in friends, evasiveness about new ones
11. Unhealthy appearance, bloodshot eyes
12. Changes in personal dress or grooming
13. Trouble with the law in or out of school
14. Unusually large appetite
15. Use of Visine, room deodorizers, incense
16. Rock group or drug-related graphics, slogans
17. Pipes, small boxes or containers, baggies, rolling papers or other unusual items
18. Peculiar odors or butts, seeds, leaves in ashtrays or clothing pockets.

WHAT PARENTS SHOULD DO IF THEIR CHILDREN ARE ON DRUGS

All the preventive measures in the world will not guarantee that our children will not experiment with drugs. If parents suspect their child is already using drugs, the following practical suggestions should be followed.

First, don't deny your suspicions. Drug addiction takes time, but occurs much faster with a child then an adult. Some of the newer drugs (especially crack) can quickly lead to addiction. Parents should act on their suspicions. Denial may waste precious time. A child's life may be in danger.

Second, learn to recognize the symptoms of drug abuse. The warning signs listed above are important clues to a child's involvement with drugs. Some readily noticeable physical symptoms include: a pale face, imprecise eye movements, and neglect of personal appearance. Some less noticeable symptoms involving social interaction include: diminished drive or reduced ambition, a significant drop in the quality of schoolwork, reduced attention span, impaired communication skills, and less care for the feelings of others.

Third, be consistent. Develop clear rules in the areas of curfew, accountability for an allowance, and where your teen spends his time. Then stick with these rules. Consistent guidelines will allow for less opportunity to stumble into sin of any kind.

Fourth, open up lines of communication with your child. Ask probing questions and become informed about the dangers of drugs and the potential risk to your child.

Finally, be tough. Fighting drugs takes patience and persistence. Don't be discouraged if you don't make headway right away. Your unconditional love is a potent weapon against drugs.

WHAT THE CHURCH CAN DO ABOUT DRUG ABUSE

The family must be the first line of defense for drugs, but an important second line of defense should be the church. The church staff and individual members can provide much-needed answers and help to those addicted to alcohol and other drugs.

Practical Suggestions for the Church Staff

First, the pastor and staff must be educated about drug abuse. Substance abuse is a medical problem, a psychological problem, and a spiritual problem. The church staff should be aware of how these various aspects of the problem interrelate. They should know the causes, effects, and treatments. They must be aware of the responses of both dependents and co-dependents. Sometimes the abuser's family prevents him from recovering by continuing to deny the problem.

The church staff can obtain good drug information through the local library and various local agencies. Fortunately, more Christians are writing good material on this issue, so check your local Christian bookstore.

Second, the congregation must be educated. The church should know the facts about substance abuse. This is a worthwhile topic for sermons and Sunday School lessons. Ignorance puts young people in particular, and the congregation in general, at risk. Christians must be armed with the facts to combat this scourge on our nation.

Third, a program of prevention must be put in place. The best way to fight drug abuse is to stop it before it starts. A program that presents the problem of substance abuse and shows the results is vital. It should also provide a biblical framework for dealing with the problem of drugs in society and in the church.

Fourth, the church might consider establishing a support group. The success of non-church-related groups like Alcoholics Anonymous points to the need for substance abusers to be in an environment that encourages acceptance and accountability.

Biblical Principles for Counseling Drug Abusers

In establishing a church program or providing counsel for a substance abuser, Christians should be aware of a number of biblical principles we should apply.

First, Christians should help the abuser see the source of his problem. It is not the drink or the drug that is ultimately the problem. Jesus said in Mark 7:18-20 that "nothing that enters a man from outside can make him 'unclean.' For it doesn't go into his heart." Instead, "What comes out of a man is what makes him 'unclean.' " Evil lies in the human heart, not in the bottle or drug.

Second, Christians must be willing to bear one another's burdens and provide comfort and counseling. Paul says in Galatians 6:1, "Brethren, even if a man is caught in any trespass, you who are spiritual, restore such a one in a spirit of gentleness; looking to yourselves, lest you too be tempted."

Third, Christians must have an understanding of the compulsive, irrational, and even violent nature of substance abuse. The Apostle Paul in his Epistle to the Romans (7:15) noted this tendency in our nature: "For that which I am doing, I do not understand; for I am not practicing what I would like to do, but I am doing the very thing I hate."

HOW SOCIETY CAN FIGHT THE DRUG PROBLEM

In addition to what the family and the church can do, society must fight America's drug epidemic on five major fronts.[28] Each one has to be successful in order to win the overall battle.

The first battlefront is at the border. Federal agents must patrol the 8,426 miles of deeply indented Florida coastline and 2,067 mile border with Mexico. This is a formidable task, but vast distances are not the only problem.

The smugglers they are up against have almost unlimited funds and some of the best equipment available. Fortunately, the federal interdiction forces (namely Customs, DEA, and INS) are improving their capabilities. Customs forces have been given an increase in officers and all are getting more sophisticated equipment.

The second battlefront is law enforcement at home. Police must crack down with more arrests, more convictions, longer sentences, and more seizures of drug dealers' assets. Unfortunately, law enforcement successes pale when compared to the volume of drug traffic. Even the most effective crackdowns seem to do little more than move drugs from one location to another.

Drug enforcement officers rightly feel both outgunned and underfunded. In the 1980s, the budget for the city of Miami's vice squad unit for an entire year was less than the cost of just one episode of the TV show "Miami Vice."[29]

An effective weapon on this battlefront is a 1984 law that makes it easier to seize the assets of drug dealers before conviction. In some cities, police have even confiscated the cars of suburbanites who drive into the city to buy crack.

But attempts to deter drug dealing have been limited by flaws in the criminal justice system. A lack of jail cells prevents significant prosecution of drug dealers. And even if this problem were alleviated, the shortage of judges would still result in the quick release of drug pushers.

A third battlefront is drug testing. Many government and business organizations are implementing testing on a routine basis in order to reduce the demand for drugs. The theory is simple. Drug testing is a greater deterrent to drug use than the remote possibility of going to jail. People who know they will have to pass a urine test in order to get a job are going to be much less likely to dabble in drugs. In 1980, 27 percent of some 20,000 military personnel admitted to using drugs in the previous 30 days. Five years later when drug testing was implemented, the proportion dropped to 9 percent.[30]

A fourth battleground is drug treatment. Those who are addicted to drugs need to be given help. But the major question is who should provide the treatment and who should foot the bill. Private hospital programs are now a $4-billion-a-year business with a daily cost of as much as $500 per bed per day. This is clearly out of the reach of many addicts who do not have employers or insurance companies who can pick up the costs.

A fifth battleground is education. Teaching children the dangers of drugs can be an important step in helping them to learn to say no to drugs. The National Institute on Drug Abuse estimates that 72 percent of the nation's elementary and secondary school children are being given some kind of drug education.[31]

The battle over drugs will continue as long as there is a demand. Families, churches, and the society at large must work to fight the scourge of drugs in our country.

NOTES

1. Elizabeth Tener, "You Can Help Kids Resist Drugs and Drinking," *McCall's*, August 1984, 92.
2. Bob Dart, "Drugs Rated Top Problem in U.S., Poll Finds," *Dallas Morning News*, 15 August 1989, 1A.
3. Jack Kelly and Sam Meddis, "Releases Poll Showing Teens Fear Drugs," *USA Today*, 14 August 1989, 3A.
4. David Lynn, "The Church's Drug of Choice," *Eternity*, November 1988, 20.
5. Ibid.
6. Russ Pulliam, "Alcoholism: Sin or Sickness?" *Christianity Today*, 18 September 1981, 22–24.
7. James R. Milan and Katherine Ketcham, *Under the Influence* (New York: Bantam, 1982), 34–37.
8. Barbara Thompson, "A Medical Expert Gives Straight Answers About a Growing Problem," *Christianity Today*, 5 August 1983, 25.
9. Constance Holden, "Genes, Personality and Alcoholism," *Psychology Today*, January 1985, 38–44.
10. L.J. West, D.S. Maxwell, E.P. Noble, and D.H. Solomon, *Annals of Internal Medicine*, 100 (1984): 405–416.
11. George Gallup, "Alcoholism's Spreading Blight," *Christianity Today*, 18 September 1981, 27.
12. Charles Leerhsen, "Alcohol and the Family," *Newsweek*, 18 January 1988, 62–68.
13. Louise Bailey Burgess, *Alcohol and Your Health* (Los Angeles: Charles Publishing Company), 41.
14. Evan Thomas, "The Enemy Within," *Time*, 15 September 1986, 62.
15. Robert Weis and Steven Mirin, *Cocaine* (New York: Ballantine Books), 1987.
16. Kurt Anderson, "Crashing on Cocaine," *Time*, 11 April 1983, 23.
17. Tom Seigfried, "Pleasure, pain: Scientists focus on cocaine's highs to unlock mysteries of addiction," *Dallas Morning News*, 11 April 1989, 12A.
18. Ibid.
19. Article by Jeffrey M. Isner in the *New England Journal of Medicine* reported in Seigfried, *Dallas Morning News*, 11 April 1989.
20. Kurt Anderson, "Crashing on Cocaine," *Time*, 11 April 1983, 25.
21. Dan Sperling, "But we are not winning on addiction," *USA To-*

day, 1 Aug. 1989, 2A.
22. Ronald Taylor, "America On Drugs," *U.S. News and World Report,* 28 July 1986, 50.
23. Merrill Unger, *Demons in the World Today* (Wheaton, Ill.: Tyndale House Publishers, 1971), 10–13, 75–76.
24. *Baker's Dictionary of Theology* (Grand Rapids, Mich.: Baker Book House, 1960), 555.
25. Charles Tate, "Work with Marijuana: II. Sensations," *Psychology Today,* May 1971.
26. Alan Watts, *The Joyous Cosmology* (New York: Vintage Books, 1962), 18–19.
27. *18 Warning Signs* (St. Petersburg, Fla.: Straight, Inc., n.d.).
28. The basic outline of this section is adapted from the article "Battle Strategies: Five Fronts in a War of Attrition" that appeared in *Time,* 15 Sept. 1986, 69–73.
29. "Harper's Index," *Harper's Magazine,* August 1985, 15.
30. "Battle Strategies," *Time,* 15 September 1986, 71.
31. Ibid., 73

7

THE PROPHETS AND SOCIAL CONCERN
J. Carl Laney

he 19th century saw the flowering of the "social gospel"[1] in America. Leading proponents Washington Gladden (1863–1918) and Walter Rauschenbusch (1861–1918) called for reformation in society and emphasized the need for churches to be concerned about the poor and the oppressed.

But the social gospel met opposition among many more traditional church leaders. There was widespread fear that participation in works of social improvement would lead to neglect of more traditional evangelistic activities. Some Christians, in effect, minimized the importance of social concerns and shared no interest in improving the conditions of suffering humanity.

Through the influence of liberation theology, the social aspect of the Gospel message has gained greater prominence today, especially in poverty-ridden Third World countries. The social gospel question was prominent at the Lausanne II conference in Manila in July 1989.[2]

What really are the social implications of biblical Christianity? Many suggest that the Gospel should include greater attention to the physical needs of the lost. Others seek to avoid compromising the "pure and simple" Gospel by social involvement and Christian activism. The purpose of this chapter is to present a biblical balance between these two approaches by looking at the Old Testament prophets. I believe they provide a scriptural pattern for addressing social concerns even though church leaders are not the prophets nor the church Old Testament Israel.

THE PROPHET AND SOCIETY

The prophets of Yahweh were raised up by God from society (Deut. 18:15) and sustained a prominent relationship with society as political and religious leaders preachers of the law, predictors of future judgment, watchmer over the spiritual life of the nation, intercessors for the people, and prosecutors against covenant-breakers. The prophets were concerned with international events and the future, while at the same time they were practical in dealing with the concerns of their own localities and generations.[3]

Kraeling has well said, "The great Hebrew prophets were public men, mainly concerned with political and social questions of the day."[4] They had a definite concern for social justice as well as religious orthodoxy. As Beecher notes, "More prominently than anything else they rebuke unequal and unkind practices in the administration of justice, and inexorably demand reformation. It is largely for the purpose of reform that they engage in public affairs."[5]

Yet while the prophets were involved in social concerns, they were not primarily *social* reformers. Bullock regards them as "theological reformers," for "their basic motivation was generated within their commitment to the fundamental laws of God."[6] Their concern for the oppressed, the widow, the orphan, the poor, and the resident alien sprang from God's own compassionate nature (Deut. 15:11; 24:14-15; Ex. 22:21-27).

Heschel has stated that justice was important to the prophets because it pertained to God's status in human life.[7] The social concern of the prophets was grounded in theological reform with an expressed concern for elevating the reputation of God and His standards in society.

The prophets considered each citizen responsible to dispense justice (Mic. 6:8). When the members of Israelite society failed to fulfill this responsibility, the prophets stepped in to interecede on behalf of those who had no intercessor. As Bullock notes, "Where the king and official, either because of apathy or inaccessibility, stepped out of their expected role, the prophets stepped in."[8]

THE PROPHET AND SOCIAL ISSUES

The prophets of Israel were greatly concerned with social issues, both moral and religious. Indeed, for the prophets, social and moral concern lay at the very heart of religion. Repeatedly they rebuked idolatry, formalistic worship, failure to support temple worship, oppression of the poor, murder, usury, and dissipation.

This social concern was not new in the prophets' day. As Kaufmann observes, "The prophetic demands for social justice echo, for the most part, the ancient covenant laws."[9] Shultz, who concurs with Kaufmann, writes:

> The ethical and social concern expressed by Moses was likewise repeatedly appealed to by the prophets. Having departed from the prescribed Mosaic standard, the Israelites were warned by the prophets of their shortcomings on the basis of the divinely revealed law of Moses.[10]

The prophets were not great innovators, presenting the Israelites with new responsibilities in the social and moral realm. Rather, they believed that the ideal for Israel's society was laid down in the covenantal legislation of the past. Justice and righteousness, the foundation of the Law and pillars of society, were viewed by the prophets as the order for every age.[11] The prophets' concern for society and social issues clearly originates with the Mosaic Law and with Yahweh Himself. The following chart illustrates that the preaching of the prophets was based on the Law:

97

Subject	Law	Prophet
The orphan and widow	Deut. 10:18	Ezek. 22:7
The return of the pledge	Ex. 22:26	Amos 2:8
The perversion of justice	Deut. 24:17	Hab. 1:4
Bribery	Ex. 23:8	Micah 3:11
Usury	Lev. 25:36	Ezek. 22:12

Many other verses relating to social concerns in the Law could be cited, including Exodus 22:21-23; Deuteronomy 14:28-29; 16:11, 14; 24:19-21; 26:12-13; 27:19. There is clearly a common body of instruction on which the messages of the prophets were based. The prophets of God simply applied the Mosaic legislation to their contemporary situations.

THE PATTERN OF THE PROPHETS

The prophets' concern for social issues is reflected throughout their writings. A brief survey illustrates this emphasis. [12]

Amos

The Prophet Amos spoke against the religious and moral corruption of his day. The sins condemned by Amos include exploitation and oppression of the poor and needy (4:1; 5:11; 8:4, 6), corrupt and degenerate religious practices (2:4, 6, 8; 4:4), corruption of justice and honesty (5:7, 10; 6:12), excessive indulgence (6:4), and disregard for the laws of God (8:5).

In dealing with the sins of Israelite society, Amos warned of impending judgment (2:5, 13-16; 3:2, 11-15; 5:25-27) and called the people to "let justice roll down like waters and righteousness like an ever-flowing stream" (5:24). The righteous person recognizes God's standard, treating others, rich or poor, equally before the Law.

Hosea

At a time of spiritual declension, God raised up Hosea to

convince Israel that the nation must repent and turn to God in order to avert divine judgment. Hosea pointed out that the root cause of the problems of the Israelites was their spiritual apostasy. Their failure toward God resulted in a failure toward fellow Israelites.

The sins of Hosea's day included harlotry (4:11, 18), false dealings (4:2; 7:1), violence and bloodshed (4:2; 6:8-9), stealing (4:2; 7:1), drunkenness (4:11; 7:5), idolatry (4:12; 8:4; 13:2), and other rebellion against God (9:15; 13:16).

The people were exhorted to repent from their sinful apostasy (6:1-3; 14:1-3) and to receive God's healing and restoration (14:4). Hosea exhorted the people to practice "love and justice" as a step along the path toward healing and restoration (12:6).

Isaiah

The sins Isaiah rebuked included idolatry (2:8; 48:5), injustice (1:21, 23; 5:7; 10:1-2; 59:8), bloodshed (5:7; 59:7), religious formalism and hypocrisy (1:10-15; 29:13; 58:1-5), rebellion (1:5; 57:4), neglect of widows and orphans (1:23; 10:2), excessive indulgence in wine and strong drink (5:11; 28:1-7), and oppression of the poor (3:14-15; 10:2).

Isaiah condemned the citizens of Judah for failing to measure up to God's righteous norms in relationship to God and others. Yet he maintained a confident expectation of the establishment of social justice. He anticipated a day in which justice and righteousness would prevail among the Israelite people.

Isaiah suggested two solutions that would enable righteousness to prevail. One was the people's repenting and doing good (1:16-17); he taught that true piety involves ceasing oppression and helping the hungry, homeless, poor, and naked. The Lord asked the people to "preserve justice, and do righteousness" (56:1). Such human efforts at righting the wrongs of society must, however, be preceded by repentance and turning to the Lord (55:6-7).

The second solution Isaiah anticipated is the coming of the

Messiah, who will establish social justice in the millennial kingdom. The Servant-Messiah will "bring forth justice to the nations" and establish "justice on the earth" (42:1, 4; cf. 2:1-4). He will establish righteousness and peace (60:17) and will effect a just rule in society through His princes (32:1). The Messiah Himself will judge the poor with righteousness and decide the case of the afflicted with fairness (11:4). A full knowledge of the Lord throughout all the earth will be the basis for harmony in the millennial society (11:9).

Micah

Micah addressed problems of the common people. He laid bare their sins, presenting God's complaints against His people. But the societal sins Micah rebuked are basically those against the common man. These include plundering and oppressing the poor and defenseless (2:2, 8-9), perversion of justice through bribery and dishonest business practices (3:11; 6:11; 7:3), idolatrous practices (1:7; 5:13-14), violence and bloodshed (6:12; 7:2), and empty religious formalism (6:6-7).

Like the Prophet Isaiah, Micah offered a twofold solution to the moral and spiritual problems of society. The first is to yield to the requirements of true religion, summed up so well in Micah 6:8: "to do justice, to love kindness, and to walk humbly with your God" (NASB). Here God linked ethics with piety.

The second aspect of the solution is the coming of the Messiah. Micah understood that individuals are responsible to provide social justice. But he recognized that the Lord is the One who will ultimately execute justice and see that relationships in society are arranged according to His divine norm. Messiah will bring peace (4:3), provide security (4:4), and free Israel from idolatry (4:5). The messianic kingdom, by virtue of Christ's rule, will yield social justice as its fruit.

Zephaniah

Zephaniah was concerned about the spiritual degeneracy of

the people, the priests, and the leaders. He condemned idolatry (1:4-5), rebellion and oppression (3:1), unbelief (3:2), and disrespect for the Law and holy things (3:4).

Repentance is the solution Zephaniah offered Judah. He exhorted the people to seek the Lord, righteousness, and humility (2:3). Such repentance would have a significant effect on the spiritual problems of the nation.

Habakkuk

Habakkuk condemned the sins of both the Judeans and their enemies the Babylonians (Chaldeans). These included violence (1:2; 2:12, 17), oppression (1:4), disregard for the Law (1:4), perversion of justice (1:4), plundering (2:8), inhumanity to man (2:10-11), and idolatry (2:18-19).

Standing on the threshold of judgment prophesied by Isaiah, Habakkuk offered no alternative to judgment (1:12). He did set forth, however, a principle of divine recompense that would function as an encouragement to the people: the upright man living in reliance on God will be preserved, whereas the proud and wicked will perish (2:4). Habakkuk anticipated a day after judgment when the knowledge of God's glory will fill the earth (2:14).

Jeremiah

Jeremiah was a prophet intensely interested in society and the religious condition of the people. The sins he rebuked included religious failure and apostasy among the people and priests (2:8, 13; 3:1; 5:31; 7:18; 17:2; 19:4-5), immorality (2:33; 3:8; 5:7-8), oppression of the poor (5:28; 7:6), and perversion of justice (7:5).

Jeremiah exhorted the people to turn from evil (4:14). Repentance from injustice, oppression, and bloodshed would deter God's judgment and would enable the faithful to enjoy God's blessing in the land. Also Jeremiah, like most of the other prophets, anticipated the coming of Messiah, who will "do justice and righteousness in the land" (23:5). Through Messiah's millennial reign, the Lord will exercise loyalty, justice, and righteousness on earth (9:24).

In addition, Jeremiah explained that the New Covenant will give the people a new basis on which to fulfill their responsibilties to God and their fellowman (31:31-34). With the law inscribed on their hearts, and a knowledge of Yahweh, the people would have divine enablement for living according to God's divine order. Jeremiah viewed the New Covenant as the spiritual solution to the social and moral problems of the people of Judah.

Ezekiel

The sins of Israelite society condemned or rebuked by Ezekiel included spiritual apostasy and idolatry (5:11; 6:3-6; 8:3, 5, 10; 14:3; 18:15; 36:18), oppression of the poor, widows, and orphans (18:12, 16; 22:29), bloodshed (22:3-4), false prophesying (13:2, 16, 23; 22:28), and sexual immorality (18:11; 22:10-11).

Ezekiel said God's judgment on Jerusalem would bring the people to a knowledge of the Lord. The phrase, "and you will know that I am the Lord," is used about 60 times in the book with reference to the expected outcome of divine judgment (6:7, 10, 13-14; 11:10, etc.). A second solution is personal repentance. Ezekiel exhorted the people to repent and live (18:30, 32). The one who turns from sin and practices righteousness "will surely live" (18:5-9; 33:14-16).

With Jeremiah, Ezekiel set forth the New Covenant as a means of bringing a new heart and understanding to the people (36:25-28). This change will serve as the spiritual basis for obedience and blessing, enabling the people to live in the righteous and just manner required by God.

Zechariah

The sins Zechariah condemned included a neglect of justice

(7:9), oppression of widows, orphans, and strangers (7:10), refusal to respond to the prophet of God (7:11), and devising evil (8:17).

The first solution Zechariah offered was repentance (1:3-4). He exhorted the people to dispense justice and practice loyalty and compassion. The people ought to speak truth, judge with truth, and love truth and peace (8:16-17, 19). Such changes in attitude and practice would help bring about social justice in Israelite society.

Like many prophets before him, Zechariah looked to the day when the Messiah will dwell in the midst of Zion, establishing a righteous and just rule in Israel (14:9-11).

Malachi

The sins of Judah in Malachi's day included corruption of religion and proper worship (Mal. 1:7-8; 3:8), perversion of justice (2:9), intermarriage with pagans (2:11), breaking the marriage covenant (2:15-16), and oppression of the helpless (3:5).

The first solution mentioned by Malachi was repentance. He exhorted the people to return to God (3:7) and obey Him (3:10; 4:4). A second solution, Malachi pointed out, is the approaching day of the Lord, in which the Messiah will come and will purge the evil and oppression from society (3:2, 17; 4:1, 3, 5-6).

THE APPLICATION OF THE STUDY

The prophets of Israel spoke to the social issues that troubled Israelite society both in matters of religious orthodoxy and social justice. The sins the prophets rebuked included the following: (1) the exploitation and oppression of the poor, orphans, widows, and aliens, (2) corrupt and degenerate religious practices, (3) idolatry and pagan practices, (4) perversion of justice, (5) dishonest business practices, (6) excessive indulgence in wine and strong drink, (7) violence of all sorts, including bloodshed and plotting evil, (8) adultery, immorality, and sexual violations, and (9) general disregard for the Law of Yahweh. This list reads like a moral commentary on contemporary society!

In response to these problems, the prophets offered four solutions. The first two relate to what man must do; the other two relate to what God will do. First, the prophets exhorted the people to repent of their evil and turn back to God (Amos 5:4-6; Hosea 6:1-3; Zeph. 2:3; Jer. 4:14). Second, the prophets exhorted the people to exercise justice, righteousness, and loyalty. They challenged the citizens of their day to take positive steps to right the wrongs of society (Amos 5:24; Isa. 1:16-17; Micah 6:8). Third, the prophets, particularly Jeremiah and Ezekiel, looked to the establishment of the New Covenant, which will provide the spiritual power for people to walk in the manner required by God (Jer. 31:31-34; Ezek. 16:60-63; 36:25-28). Fourth, the prophets anticipated the coming of the Messiah, who will establish justice and righteousness during His millennial reign (Isa. 11:4; 42:1-4; Micah 4:2-4).

The prophets of Israel and Judah did not cloister themselves from society and its problems. They were aware of the issues and were actively involved in speaking to the social and moral concerns of their day. They pointed out social injustice and rebuked it as sin. They called on the Israelites to do something personally to correct the evils in their society. They had confidence that the New Covenant would give God's people the power and resources to work actively toward the establishing of social justice, and yet they recognized that complete justice and righteousness would ultimately be established by the Messiah in His future kingdom. A survey of the Gospels indicates that Jesus adhered closely to this pattern (Matt. 4:17; 5:3-12; 26:20-29; Luke 3:10-14; John 5:14).

Some may object to setting forth the prophets as models for Christians in confronting social and moral issues. Admittedly the church is not Israel, and pastors are not biblical prophets. Yet what is modeled by the prophets is certainly underscored in the New Testament Epistles. Paul instructed the Galatians,

"Let us not lose heart in doing good. . . . So then, while we have opportunity, let us do good to all men, and especially to those who are of the household of faith" (Gal. 6:9-10). The writer of Hebrews admonished, "Do not neglect doing good and sharing; for with such sacrifices God is pleased" (Heb. 13:16). James wrote of visiting "orphans and widows in their distress" (James 1:27) and he described good works as expressions of a genuine faith: "Faith by itself, if it is not accompanied by action, is dead" (2:15-17). Therefore, it seems that the principles reflected in the prophets are not limited to a particular dispensation.

The Old Testament prophets provide a splendid pattern and an impetus for confronting and dealing with the sins and injustices of modern society. Like the prophets, Christians today should (1) recognize and condemn sin, (2) call men and women to repent of their sin, (3) direct men and women to Christ for the regeneration of the human heart and the New Covenant empowerment to overcome sin, (4) exhort people to take positive steps to correct wrongs and injustice, and (5) anticipate the return of Christ, who will establish perfect justice and righteousness during His reign in the millennium.

The prophets balanced spiritual and physical concerns, recognizing both man's part and God's part in the ultimate solution to each. This balance is reflected in the words of Amy Carmichael. Speaking in response to criticism of her humanitarian work in India, she said, "One cannot save and then pitchfork souls into heaven. . . . Souls are more or less securely fastened to bodies . . . and as you cannot get the souls out and deal with them separately, you have to take them both together."[13]

Christians must not be content to be experts on what the Bible says about contemporary social and moral issues. Following the pattern of the prophets, they should actively engage in confronting sin and injustice, directing the repentant to salvation in Christ. Seeking to right wrongs and help the oppressed, Christians may enjoy the assurance that Christ is coming again to complete the task.

NOTES

1. For a helpful summary article, see *The International Dictionary of the Christian Church,* ed. J.D. Douglas (1974), "Social Gospel," by Roy H. Campbell, 911.

2. "Global Camp Meeting," *Christianity Today,* 18 August 1989, 39–40.

3. Willis Judson Beecher, *The Prophets and the Promise* (New York: Thomas Y. Cromwell Co., 1905), 98.

4. Emil G. Kraeling, *The Prophets* (New York: Rand McNally & Co., 1969), 15.

5. Beecher, *The Prophets and the Promise,* 97.

6. C. Hassell Bullock, *An Introduction to the Old Testament Prophetic Books* (Chicago: Moody Press, 1986), 25.

7. Abraham J. Heschel, *The Prophets,* 2 vols. (New York: Harper & Row, 1962), 1:198.

8. Bullock, *Old Testament Prophetic Books,* 25.

9. Yehezkel Kaufmann, *The Religion of Israel,* trans. Moshe Greenberg (London: George Allen & Unwin, 1960), 365.

10. Samuel J. Shultz, *The Prophets Speak* (New York: Harper & Row Publishers, 1968), 36.

11. Bullock, *Old Testament Prophetic Books,* 19.

12. Though the theme of social concern is reflected throughout the prophets, three Major Prophets (Isaiah, Jeremiah, and Ezekiel) and seven Minor Prophets (Hosea, Amos, Micah, Habakkuk, Zephaniah, Zechariah, and Malachi) illustrate this emphasis.

13. Quoted by Ruth A. Tucker in *Guardians of the Great Commission* (Grand Rapids: Zondervan Publishing House, 1988), 134.

■ ■ ■ ■ ■ ■ ■ ■ ■

LEGAL
ISSUES

8

LIVING IN TWO WORLDS
John A. Witmer

P hilip Nolan is the hero of Edward Everett Hale's classic American short story, "The Man without a Country." According to this story, Philip Nolan was an eager young officer in the Western army under Aaron Burr in the first decade of the 19th century. Burr was plotting a rebellion against the United States of America to set up a separate government west of the Appalachians. The youthful members of his staff, including Nolan, were duped into becoming unwitting partners in the plot. It was discovered, of course, and all those implicated were court-martialed. Still convinced Burr was a hero instead of a traitor, Nolan impetuously told the court he never wanted to see the flag of the United States again. He lived to regret that rash vow and to become a fervent patriot, but the verdict of the court was that his wish be carried out. For the rest of his life he was shunted from one naval vessel to another, never to set foot on American soil and never to see the Stars and Stripes again. He was truly a man without a country.

Hale told his story so artfully that many people thought it was true, that there really was a Philip Nolan who was sailing the seven seas as the man without a country. Their sympathies aroused, many wrote to Washington demanding Nolan's pardon. They felt that because he had regretted his vow he should be allowed back in America. But the story was fiction.

THE CHRISTIAN'S CITIZENSHIP

The subject of this chapter, however, is not fiction. It is somewhat the reverse of Hale's story about Philip Nolan, because it is the record of the man with two countries. Each Christian is this man with two countries, because the child of God through faith in the Lord Jesus Christ is a citizen of the kingdom of God and also a citizen of an earthly nation and government. Christians hold citizenship in two lands—one temporal and physical, the other eternal and spiritual. Many of the problems Christians face grow out of the interrelationships and the conflicts of priority between these two citizenships. Therefore it is appropriate to consider what the Bible teaches about the man with two countries, the Christian citizen.

The scriptural witness to the heavenly citizenship of Christians builds on a number of passages. First in importance is Philippians 3:20, where Paul reminded the Philippian Christians, "Our citizenship is in heaven." The Greek word translated "citizenship" is a word that may be translated "citizenship, community, commonwealth."[1] The scholar Moffat renders this clause, "We are a colony of heaven."[2]

A related word occurs in Philippians 1:27, which reads, "Conduct yourselves in a manner worthy of the gospel." The verb for "conduct yourselves" can be rendered "live as a citizen." The use of these words in Paul's correspondence to the Philippians is significant and appropriate, since the city prided itself on being a Roman colony.

Another passage that relates to the heavenly citizenship of the believer is Colossians 1:12-13, which reads, "Giving thanks to the Father, who has qualified you to share in the inheritance of the saints in the kingdom of light. For he has rescued us from the dominion of darkness and brought us into the kingdom of the Son he loves." In verse 13 the Greek word translated "dominion" has the concept of "authority." God delivered believers from the authority (or sphere of dominion) of the satanic realm of darkness, where men are held as slaves in unbelief and spiritual death. Furthermore, God has translated believers "into the kingdom of the Son He loves."

In Ephesians, Paul described Gentiles prior to their spiritual identification with Jesus Christ as "excluded from citizenship in Israel" (2:12), the circle of divine covenantal blessing. As a result of their position in Jesus Christ by grace through faith, however, Gentile believers "are no longer foreigners and aliens, but fellow citizens with God's people" (Eph. 2:19). Added to these major passages affirming the Christian's citizenship in heaven are the numerous references to "the kingdom of Christ and of God" (Eph. 5:5) and the fact that entrance into it is only by being "born again" (John 3:3, 5, 7).

The Christian's other citizenship, that in an earthly nation, is obvious. Surprisingly, some cultists deny it, insisting that Christians have only a spiritual citizenship. The Scriptures, however, present the Christian's earthly citizenship as an important part of his life. When Paul and Silas were beaten and imprisoned in Philippi (Acts 16:23) on the second missionary journey, it was without proper trial and judgment. This was illegal treatment of Roman citizens, which Paul and Silas were (16:37). When Paul revealed the fact of their Roman citizenship the next morning, the magistrates "were alarmed" and treated them with deference (16:38-39). Paul knew his rights as a Roman citizen and he demanded that they be observed.

Paul made a similar issue of his Roman citizenship at the close of his third missionary journey in Jerusalem. Rescued from the Jewish mob intent on killing him, Paul was taken into protective custody by Roman soldiers. After his address to the mob ended in a violent uproar, the commander ordered Paul flogged to secure a confession of guilt from him (Acts 22:24). As he was being bound, Paul asked the centurion, "Is it legal for you to flog a Roman citizen who hasn't even been found guilty?" (22:25). The centurion warned the commander of Paul's status, who came to confirm the fact for himself (22:26-27). When the commander boasted that he had purchased Roman citizenship with "a big price," Paul replied with quiet pride, "I was born a Roman citizen" (22:28). Paul valued the fact that he was a Roman citizen. The New Testament sees no necessary conflict between being a good citizen of heaven and a good citizen of an earthly government at the same time.[3]

Since the Christian as the man with two countries must fulfill his responsibilities in both realms simultaneously, tensions are bound to occur over priorities and God's will for him as an individual. In addition, some Christians take stances on the believer's relationship to his earthly citizenship that are unbiblical extremes. At least four such positions can be identified. Instead of easing the tensions of living in two kingdoms at once, these views aggravate them.

UNBIBLICAL EXTREMES

Blind Nationalism

Basically, the view of blind nationalism is what much of the current discussion about civil religion is warning against. In this view, the biblical principle of the divine ordination of human government (Rom. 13:1-2) is emphasized to the point that it is not even subject to God's moral law and government. Blind nationalism is expressed in the slogan "My country, right or wrong!" It is illustrated by Hitler's Third Reich. If the Christians of Germany had opposed Hitler's unbiblical philosophy of Aryan superiority and his persecution of Jews, the bloodbath of World War II may not have occurred. Christians can be patriots, but they must always judge the policies and programs of their government and its leaders by the standards of the Word of God.

World Citizenship

At the opposite end of the spectrum from blind nationalism is the unbiblical extreme of world citizenship. This position considers national governments as unnecessary anachronisms from humanity's past. Advocates of this view argue that instant worldwide television viewing via space satellite and supersonic world transportation confront all men with their common bond and common destiny as inhabitants of Spaceship Earth. As a result, one-world enthusiasts insist that multiplied national states are potentially dangerous and expendable luxuries. Men should renounce their national citizenships and support a world government. Patriotism is demeaned or even branded as evil.

Some aspects of this position possess validity. It is true that "from one man [God] made every nation of men, that they should inhabit the whole earth" (Acts 17:26). It is also true that increasingly the welfare of all living men is inseparably bound together. Furthermore, the Bible does support world government: "the kingdom of the world has become the kingdom of our Lord and of his Christ" (Rev. 11:15). But this messianic world government will be inaugurated by the omnipotence of God, not by man's political charisma, organizational genius, or cooperative spirit. The only other worldwide government on earth described in Scripture is that of Satan's counterfeit, the beast, the man of sin (Rev. 13; 2 Thes. 2:3-4), who will be destroyed by the returning Lord Jesus Christ (2 Thes. 2:8; Rev. 19:19-21).

National states as they existed in biblical times and today are not contrary to the will of God. As a matter of fact, God was directly responsible for creating the nation of Israel (Deut. 7:6-8), if not all nations. Patriotism, therefore, and love of country are not sinful. As already noted, the Apostle Paul valued his Roman citizenship and was justly proud of it.

Civic Irresponsibility

The third unbiblical position in the relationship between heavenly citizenship and earthly citizenship is what can be called civic irresponsibility. This view stresses the priority of spiritual citizenship to the point of virtual denial of citizenship in an earthly government. At least the civic responsibilities of citizenship are denied. Adherents of this view will not salute the flag or pledge allegiance to it, will not vote in elections nor hold office, and will not serve in the armed forces or even register for military service. They insist that they are citizens of heaven and have no responsibility to any earthly government. Though quick to shun the responsibilities of earthly citizenship, are usually just as quick to demand the rights of citizenship when they are threatened.

Civic Indifference

The fourth unbiblical view is civic indifference. It has two forms. The first can be termed political isolationism. These Christians pay their taxes and support the police and serve in the armed forces when required. But they refuse to take part in the political process on any level because "politics is dirty." They fail to realize that if their indictment of politics is correct, it is so in part because they as "the salt of the earth" (Matt. 5:13) and as "the light of the world" (5:14) have withdrawn from it.

The second form of civic indifference can be called political ignorance. These Christians are not involved in the processes of government beyond casting their vote in national elections, if they even do that. When they vote, they are basically uninformed about issues or candidates. They excuse their lack of participation by being preoccupied with spiritual affairs. They are contributing to the low state of politics by their indifference and are violating the intent of Scripture, which instructs Christians to "honor the king" (1 Peter 2:17) and to make "requests, prayers, intercession, and thanksgiving . . . for kings, and all those in authority" (1 Tim. 2:1-2). These commands are impossible to fulfill properly without knowledge of the affairs of state and of the people who fill the offices of government.

CONFLICTS IN HEAVENLY AND EARTHLY REALMS

God intends that the Christian should live as the man with two countries without conflict in fulfilling his responsibilities in both realms. Tensions of priority and of emphasis may develop from time to time, but normally direct conflict between the two realms and their demands on the believer will not occur. Whenever such conflict does occur, however, the kingdom of God and its requirements are to take precedence over the earthly governments and their demands. God and His kingdom are ultimate. At such junctures the Christian must simply say with Peter and the apostles, "We must obey God rather than men" (Acts 5:29, NASB).

The Bible gives several examples of such conflict between the edicts of earthly governments and the spiritual requirements of God. In every case the earthly authority demanded something God prohibited or forbade something God required. The three Hebrew young men—Shadrach, Meshach, and Abednego—refused to bow down to the gold image Nebuchadnezzar had erected, being willing to suffer death in the fiery furnace rather than compromise their worship of Yahweh, the one true God (Dan. 3). Daniel refused to stop his practice of praying to Yahweh and praising Him three times a day when Darius decreed no petition be made to any god or man except him for 30 days. In fact, Daniel not only refused to stop praying to the Lord but also continued to pray in his open window in plain view of all who passed his house (Dan. 6). During the reign of the beast in the end time, many will be martyred for their faith in Jehovah and their refusal to worship the beast and his image (Rev. 13:15; 6:10-11; 20:4).

Related to this issue is the persecution of the apostles and early Christians, recorded in the Book of Acts. This persecution did not arise from an earthly civil government, but from the religious authority and hierarchy of the Jews. Except for the isolated cases of Herod's execution of James the brother of John (Acts 12:1-2) and Herod's imprisonment of Peter (12:3-19), the Roman government took no part in the persecution and martyrdom of Christians until after the history as recorded in Acts ends. But the Jewish leaders in Jerusalem, seeking to suppress the burgeoning sect of the Nazarene, used their quasi-official authority to forbid Peter and John to speak or teach "in the name of Jesus" (4:18). The two apostles responded, "Judge for yourselves whether it is right in God's sight to obey you rather than God. For we cannot help speaking about what we have seen and heard" (4:19-20).

Daniel, his three friends, the apostles, and the myriad of Christian martyrs throughout church history willingly endured imprisonment, persecution, and even death for their determination to obey God rather than men. In the modern phenomenon of civil disobedience, however, many who defy national, state, and local laws in the name of religion or conscience seem to expect exemption from the consequences of their defiance. They apparently think that religion or conscience is a justifiable reason for breaking the law.

A good illustration of this attitude occurred during the Vietnam conflict. The government provided an alternative service program for sincere conscientious objectors. Many took advantage of that option. Many others, however, refused to register for the draft or burned their draft cards and then sought pardon from the penalty of their actions. Others hid in remote areas of this country or fled to Canada or other countries. After the conflict ended, they demanded amnesty because they had obeyed their consciences, which all too often were sensitive only on the Vietnam conflict. Civil disobedience at times may be necessary, but I believe that those who do so should accept their punishment for breaking the law without complaint. This applies to pro-life advocates who block entrances to clinics and harass patrons and then protest arrest by the police.

In democratic countries, civil disobedience or acquiescence to unjust or bad laws are not the only alternatives for the Christian. Democratic governments provide proper avenues for changing laws. They can be altered through remedial legislation. In addition, laws can be challenged through the courts. But no citizen, even the Christian, has the right to set himself up as legislature or as supreme court to decide which laws he will obey and which he will not obey without being willing to accept the punishment for his disobedience. When the individ-

116

ual's conscience has authority over law, then government by law is jeopardized. At that point a nation is logically only one step removed from the condition of Israel when "everyone did as he saw fit" (Jud. 17:6; 21:25). Sooner or later anarchy rules.

THE CHRISTIAN'S RESPONSIBILITIES TO GOVERNMENT

What positive direction does the Bible give the Christian as the man with two countries on how to relate properly to earthly government? The Scriptures include a wealth of material on the Christian's responsibilities to the nation of which he is a citizen. This teaching is found not only in Romans 13—undoubtedly the classic passage on the subject—but also in 1 Timothy, 1 Peter, the teaching of the Lord Jesus as recorded in the Gospels, and in the Old Testament. At least five distinct responsibilities can be delineated in the Bible. Of these, four are commands from God through apostolic spokesmen and one is an option by example.

Respect

Perhaps logically the first responsibility of the Christian citizen toward his earthly government is expressed in Peter's command, "Honor the king" (1 Peter 2:17). This is the responsibility to respect the government. The Apostle Paul echoed this command when he wrote, "Give everyone what you owe him . . . if respect, then respect, if honor, then honor" (Rom. 13:7). The Greek verb translated "honor" has the commercial sense of "to fix the value." The basis for respect for government and those who exercise its authority is Paul's explanation that "there is no authority except that which God has established" (Rom. 13:1). This is supported by Daniel's teaching and Nebuchadnezzar's lesson that "the Most High is sovereign over the kingdoms of men and gives them to anyone he wishes" (Dan. 4:17, 25, 35).

Peter and Paul gave their commands to the apostolic Christians when Nero was emperor of Rome. Few men were more despicable than Nero. Honor and respect are due to the office the man holds, not necessarily to the man who holds the office. Paul illustrated this principle when the high priest Ananias commanded him to be smitten on the mouth. Paul responded by calling him a "whitewashed wall" (Acts 23:3) who perverted Jewish justice. When Paul learned that Ananias was high priest, he said, "Brothers, I did not realize that he was the high priest; for it is written, 'Do not speak evil about the ruler. of your people' " (23:5).

Daniel rightly said that God sets over the kingdom of men "the lowliest of men" (Dan. 4:17), but respect for the office or position of authority is commanded nonetheless.

Submission

The Christian citizen's second responsibility to earthly government is submission, or obedience. Peter stated it as a command: "Submit yourselves for the Lord's sake to every authority instituted among men: whether to the king as the supreme authority or governors, who are sent by him" (1 Peter 2:13-14). Paul exhorted, "Everyone must submit himself to the governing authorities" (Rom. 13:1). This was repeated when he wrote, "Remind the people to be subject to rulers and authorities, to be obedient" (Titus 3:1). In all three passages the same verb is used, which means "to place or rank under" another. That same verb *submit* is used of the Christian's responsibility to obey God (James 4:7). Paul placed the responsibility on every person, and Peter extends it to every ordinance.

One obvious reason for obedience to civil government and its laws is found in Paul's statement "for he does not bear the sword for nothing" (Rom. 13:4). One significant function of civil government is to maintain law and order by punishing those who do evil and by protecting those who do good (Rom. 13:3-4; 1 Peter 2:14). But both Paul and Peter also presented

118

a higher reason for such obedience, a spiritual reason. Paul wrote, "Therefore, it is necessary to submit to the authorities, not only because of possible punishment but also because of conscience" (Rom. 13:5). This is because the civil authorities are "God's servant" (13:4), as Paul stated twice. Peter's words are even stronger. He commanded, "Submit yourselves for the Lord's sake . . . for it is God's will" (1 Peter 2:13, 15). It is part of the Christian's responsibility as a citizen of heaven to be obedient as a citizen of an earthly government.

Support

The third responsibility of the Christian to his earthly government is that of support, financial and otherwise. In a sense, this grows logically out of the second responsibility, for maintaining law and order is one of the services government provides for its citizens. Such services must be paid for. Imperial Rome is legendary for its Pax Romana and Lex Romana — peace and law. She is also famous for the network of roads that spanned the empire, remnants of which remain today. And there were the aqueducts, the theaters, the stadiums, the hippodromes, and the public buildings that Rome built. All these things cost money in ancient Rome even as they do today. The only form of government financing is taxation of its citizens in various ways.

Basic to the biblical teaching on the Christian's responsibility to support civil government is the dictum of the Lord Jesus Christ, "Give to Caesar what is Caesar's" (Mark 12:17; cf. Matt. 22:21; Luke 20:25). Representatives of the Pharisees and Herodians had come to Jesus seeking to trap Him in His words (Mark 12:13). Their question was, "Is it right to give taxes to Caesar or not?" (12:14). They thought they had Him caught on the horns of a dilemma. If He answered yes, He would lose favor with the common people who longed for freedom from Rome's rule. If He answered no, He could be accused of sedition. Jesus simply asked for a denarius coin and then asked whose portrait and inscription appeared on it

(12:16). When they responded, "Caesar's," He told them to pay back to Caesar what belonged to him. His point is that the services of government cost money which must be paid for by taxes. Paul supported this teaching when he wrote, "This is why you pay taxes" (Rom. 13:6). He commanded, "Give everyone what you owe him: If you owe taxes, pay taxes; if revenue, then revenue; if respect, then respect; if honor, then honor" (13:7).

Participation

The responsibility to support civil government financially leads logically to the fourth responsibility the Christian has as a citizen of an earthly nation, which is participation. This responsibility is not directly commanded in Scripture, but it is clearly presented by outstanding examples such as Joseph and Daniel. Joseph did not refuse Pharaoh's offer of a high position by saying he was a spiritual man who did not get involved in politics. Instead, he accepted the job and delivered not only Egypt but also his own family from famine. Daniel was a young man of royal Hebrew blood. He became a man of high position in both the empires of Babylon and Persia under the blessing and leadership of the Lord. As far as Scripture records, the Ethiopian treasurer (Acts 8), Cornelius the centurion (Acts 9), Sergius Paulus, the deputy of Cyprus (Acts 13), and the Philippian jailer (Acts 16) did not resign their government positions when they became Christians. The normal assumption is that they continued to serve, but also as citizens of heaven.

The responsibility for participation in civil government falls on every Christian to some degree. It may be no more than participation through financial support, discussed above. In democratic governments it certainly involves participation by voting at elections for all levels of government. To do this faithfully as a Christian requires being informed on the policies and issues that are being decided and concerning the candidates who are offering themselves for public office. To this point at least, participation as a citizen in civil government is incumbent on every Christian as a spiritual concern.

Beyond the point of informed voting, participation in the political process of government is an individual matter requiring direction from the Lord. God may lead many Christians to do nothing more. He may direct many to become involved in a political party at the precinct, district, county, state, or national level. He may guide some to offer themselves as candidates for public office at various levels and to serve if elected. This is a matter of personal guidance of the individual Christian by the Lord. Great need exists for Christians to be involved in the political process as "the salt of the earth" and "the light of the world" (Matt. 5:13-14), but the direction must come from God to the individual. Doing the will of God is just as basic in this area as in any other.

Prayer

The final responsibility of the Christian as a citizen of an earthly government is prayer—faithful, fervent, specific, daily prayer. The Apostle Paul writes, "I urge, then, first of all, that requests, prayers, intercessions, and thanksgiving be made for kings, and all those in authority" (1 Tim. 2:1-2). In this entreaty Paul used four generally synonymous words that have specific emphases. *Requests* have to do with specific needs related to government for which divine help is requested. *Prayers* is the general word used only of petitions to God. *Intercessions* relates to the idea of conversation and petition. The fourth, *thanksgiving,* conveys the necessity for thanks and praise to God.

Paul then presented two reasons for this exhortation to pray for government leaders. The first is "that we may live peaceful and quiet lives in all godliness and holiness" (1 Tim. 2:2). This raises the question as to how much of the turmoil of national life is the result of failure by Christians to pray for government leaders.

The second reason is that God desires that government leaders become Christians. Paul continued, "God our Saviour

121

. . . wants all men to be saved and to come to a knowledge of the truth" (1 Tim. 2:3-4).

God has called the believer in the Lord Jesus Christ into the unique position of being "the man with two countries." God desires the Christian to function to His glory as both a citizen of heaven and a citizen of an earthly country. Problems and tensions will exist, and perhaps even direct conflict will develop; but God has provided guidelines in the Scriptures, and by the Holy Spirit He will lead the believer to live in both realms to the fulfillment of His will.

NOTES

1. G. Abbott-Smith, *A Manual Greek Lexicon of the New Testament,* 3d ed. (Edinburgh: T. & T. Clark, 1937), 371.
2. James Moffat, *A New Translation of the Bible Containing the Old and New Testaments* (New York: Harper & Bros., 1954).
3. One additional passage of Scripture relates to this phase of the subject. The day after his protective arrest by the Roman authorities in Jerusalem, Paul was brought before the Jewish Sanhedrin to hear the accusations against him (Acts 22:30). Paul spoke to the council as follows, "My brothers, I have fulfilled my duty to God in all good conscience to this day" (23:1). The words "I have fulfilled my duty" translate the same as the words used in Philippians 1:27, which more literally mean "I have lived as a citizen." The problem is deciding whether Paul is referring to his spiritual citizenship as a child of God or to his earthly citizenship as a Jew. Commentators differ. Those who choose spiritual citizenship stress the phrase "before God," while adherents to earthly citizenship point out that Paul was speaking to the Jewish council to defend himself against charges of breaking both the Mosaic Law and Jewish custom. Instead of choosing one view over another, perhaps the best solution is to accept both.

9
THE PURPOSE OF PENOLOGY IN THE MOSAIC LAW AND TODAY
Gary R. Williams

Here's a riddle: What degrades, dehumanizes, criminalizes, embitters men against society, and is supported by the United States taxpayer?

According to many people, the culprit that answers that description is the prison-centered penal-correctional system. Attention has been most dramatically drawn to penological woes through the rash of prison strikes, demonstrations, riots, and killings. But prisoners are not the only ones dissatisfied with the U.S. prison system. David A. Ward speaks of the extent of the concern when he says,

> In addition to inmate leaders and "radicals," citizens have heard the President, the Chief Justice of the Supreme Court, the attorney general, their own governors, and other public figures condemn prisons as "schools for crime" and "correctional institutions that don't correct." The most common theme at the national conferences of American correctional administrators has become "The Crisis in Corrections."[1]

The solutions to these problems in our prisons are not easily ascertainable, though simplistic solutions are often heard proclaimed with dogmatism from all points on the penological spectrum. "The sad fact [is] that almost everything we do in the criminal justice field is on the basis of faith, and . . . there is generally no more empirical support for continuing what is being done than there is for changing."[2]

With this being the status of penology today, one could wish for a direct word from God on how to deal with convicted offenders. Though no such word has been given directly to any modern society, the Bible does record in some detail a civil law given to ancient Israel by the all-wise God. While that law is not applicable in every detail to modern pluralistic society, it certainly provides a superb starting point for finding answers to today's penological riddles.

Penological philosophy generally has been shaped by one or more of the following four purposes: retribution, deterrence, restraint, and rehabilitation. There is no unanimity today on which of these purposes ought to predominate. The disagreement is especially acute in light of the evidence that there are numerous functional contradictions inherent in any attempt both to punish with fairness and to rehabilitate with understanding, contradictions which are likely to result in failure to achieve either end.[3]

It is the purpose of this chapter to compare the objectives of modern penology[4] with those of the God-given Mosaic Law[5] in order to shed some light on the direction in which penological philosophy should be moving to solve some of its current conundrums.

RETRIBUTION

Retribution, the principle of punishing the criminal, is not popular in current penological literature. A typical modern position designates as "uninformed" those who approve retribution as a guiding principle.[6] Others concede that there may be some value to retribution but reject it as unworthy of an enlightened society.[7]

On the other hand, God's law given to Israel was pervaded by the principle of retribution. Perhaps the clearest statement of this principle was found in what is called the *lex talionis*—life for life, eye for eye, etc. (Ex. 21:23-25; Lev. 24:17-21)—but it underlay many other regulations in the Mosaic Law as well (e.g., Deut. 19:16-21; 22:24; 25:5-12).

For at least two reasons, God included a heavy emphasis on retribution in the law, neither of which is without validity today. First, the stress on retribution taught something about God, namely, that He, being just, requires punishment for sin. It also taught something about man, namely, that he is responsible for what he does—an idea that is unpopular today.[8]

Actually, the functioning of our correctional system includes far more retribution than one would be led to believe by the rehabilitation rhetoric of both theoreticians and administrators. The punitive nature of criminal law and court decisions and the high priority given by the general public to the goal of punishment necessitate a certain degree of retribution orientation in modern correctional systems. Interestingly, some authorities, recognizing the incompatability of punishment and treatment goals, advocate a return to a system in which fixed penalties are administered to fit the crime and where there is no formal obligation to rehabilitate offenders.[9]

DETERRENCE

The concept of deterrence—crime prevention through fear of punishment—has not fared much better in current penological literature than has retribution. Some would go so far as to identify "the belief in punishment as deterrence as the greatest single obstacle in the development of efficient methods of penology,"[10] or to suggest that "it may be doubted whether one murderer ever stayed his hand, or one burglar kept away from an inviting haul, simply because he knew that if he was caught he would go to prison or worse."[11] It must be admitted that there is evidence that incarceration is not significantly valuable in reducing crime.[12]

Again in contrast to the current trend, the God-given Mosaic Law stated with reference to at least three offenses that administering the prescribed punishment would result in a public hearing, fear, and the determination never again to commit such a crime (Deut. 13:11; 17:13; 19:20; 21:21). How are we to explain the discrepancy between these passages and current evidence concerning the effectiveness of punishment as a crime deterrent? The answer probably lies in four significant differences between the punishments prescribed by God and those in vogue today.

First, the punishments prescribed by the Mosaic Law were more unpleasant than those exacted today. The major modern penal form is incarceration. Capital punishment has been used sparingly in recent years, and now hardly at all. Although prison life is far from pleasant, it is not an unmixed horror, and some of its most disagreeable aspects are soon forgotten by the ex-inmate when he encounters the difficulty of reentering the outside world.[13] In the Mosaic Law, incarceration was almost nonexistent. There punishment was primarily either fiscal or physical. Heavy fines were levied for a number of offenses (Ex. 21:18-19; 22:17; Lev. 24:18; Num. 5:6-8; Deut. 22:13-19, 25-29). Almost all other offenses called for either beating (Deut. 25:1-3), mutilation (Ex. 21:22-25; Lev. 24:19-20; Deut. 25:11-12), or death.[14]

Even when the death penalty has been exacted in modern times in the United States, the mode of execution has not been as unpleasant as that required by the Mosaic Law. Hanging, lethal gas, and electrocution are relatively painless ways to die. Two modes of execution were specified in the Mosaic Law: death at the hand of the blood avenger (Num. 35:16-21, 26-27; Deut. 19:11-12) and death by stoning (Lev. 20:2, 27; Num. 15:32-36; Deut. 13:6-10; 17:2-5; 21:18-21; 22:13-21), neither of which would have been as painless as present-day methods.

While the Mosaic penalties were severe enough to arouse fear, they were not without their humane limitations. Beatings were limited to 40 strokes to protect the dignity of the beaten as much as his health (Deut. 25:3). Mutilation, although quite common throughout history for a variety of offenses,[15] was administered only for the crime of mutilating another person. The Babylonian law calling for the amputation of the right hand of the physician whose patient died during surgery[16] would have been out of place in the Mosaic Law, as well as torture administered to secure information or confessions. Even the penalty of death by stoning was not as dreadful as some of the barbarous techniques used by other nations of antiquity, such as the Persian and Assyrian mode of driving a stake into the body and thus impaling it.[17] Kenneth Kitchen notes that because the Mosaic Law placed a supreme value on human life, its penalties for homicide were more severe and its penalties for property offenses less severe than those found in Babylonian law.[18]

A second reason why Mosaic punishments were expected to deter from crime was that they were more public than those assessed today. The punishment of incarceration is experienced almost hidden from the public eye, and executions in recent years have been observed by only a handful of witnesses. In contrast, under the Mosaic Law the public not only observed but also actually carried out the execution of convicted offenders (Lev. 20:2; 24:10-16, 23; Num. 15:32-36; Deut. 13:6-9; 17:2-7; 21:18-21; 22:13-21). Occasionally the body was even subjected to postmortem burning or hanging, making the awfulness of the death penalty further publicized.

Third, the Mosaic punishments were swifter than are today's penological measures. That is, the time between the apprehension of an offender and the execution of his punishment was not so long then. There are at least two points at which the penal process is often greatly delayed. The first is the period between the apprehension of the criminal and his coming to trial. Edith Flynn, commenting on the current excessive duration of pretrial detention, observes, "To judge from the vast delays and judicial backlogs, few seem to heed the advice of classic criminal law that in order for justice to be effective, it must be swift."[19] The fact that the Mosaic Law called for thorough investigation (Deut. 17:4; 19:18) indicates that cases were not to be unduly rushed into court. However, the lack of legal room for the kind of delaying maneuvers that are so commonly employed by the defense today[20] and the provision for sufficient courts to eliminate judicial backlogs (Ex. 18:13-26; Deut. 1:9-17; 16:18) must have greatly shortened pretrial detention. The success and growing use of United States small-claims courts is evidence that judicial backlogs can be reduced and justice administered much more swiftly than it often is today.[21]

A second point at which the penal process is often delayed today is the period between the conviction of the offender and his punishment. Truman Capote, writing 11 years ago, noted that "in the disposition of capital cases in the United States, the median elapsed time between sentence and execution is approximately seventeen months."[22] At the time of Capote's writing two rapists in Louisiana had been waiting a record 12 years.[23] The main reason for these lengthy delays is our system of appeals designed to protect the rights of the accused. The capital case about which Capote wrote was carried all the way to the United States Supreme Court three times before its convicted murderers were executed.[24]

Such a time-consuming appeals process did not exist in the Mosaic Law. Cases at times were to be carried to a supreme court, but not because the parties to the case requested it. Rather, they were brought to the high court when the judges of the lower courts were not able to arrive at a decision (Deut. 1:17; 17:8-12).

Fourth, the punishments under the Mosaic Law were more certain than they are today. Flynn believes that "the effectiveness of general deterrence, which has as its object the public as a whole, seems more a function of certainty than of severity of punishment."[25] Miriam DeFord is in agreement when she objects to the belief in punishment as deterrence on the ground that most criminals do not expect to be caught and convicted.[26] The closer-knit fabric of society in ancient Israel must have made detection and arrest harder to avoid. Once an offender was arrested—if indeed he was an offender, for there were provisions in the Mosaic Law to protect the rights of the accused (e.g., Ex. 23:6-8; Deut. 1:16-17; 16:18-20; 17:6; 19:15-21)—his conviction and punishment were definitely more certain than they are today. The role of the blood avenger, the concept that the punishment should fit the crime rather than the criminal, and the absence of both an appeals process and suspended sentences all contributed to a certainty of suffering for the offender.

Punishment, then, under the Mosaic Law was characterized by more severity, publicity, swiftness, and certainty than it is today, and God expected such punishment to deter from crime. It should be noted that in spite of the claims by some today that punishment cannot deter, there is good evidence that when properly applied it does. DeFord insists that belief in punishment as deterrence is ignorance, but she cites empirical evidence that destroys her argument:

> Reputedly, no Japanese prisoner has ever escaped. In earthquakes and other emergencies, prisoners who cannot be transferred to a safe place are set free for 24 hours, few fail to give themselves up again, as both they and those who helped them are subject to severe penalties if they do so.[27]

RESTRAINT

Restraint, the isolation of the offender in order to protect the community, is accepted by most today as a valid penological purpose. It is one of the reasons imprisonment is almost the only sentence given for felonies.

However, restraint as it is currently understood was not found in the Mosaic Law. The closest thing to imprisonment was the cities of refuge, and their purpose was not the protection of society from the offender, but vice versa. In a sense, the principle of restraint was found in the provisions for judicial mutilation, a punishment which identified the offender to the community as a violent person. However, the main means of protecting the community from dangerous criminals was capital punishment. Apparently capital punishment was also applied to those whose offenses, though not dangerous, were stubbornly habitual (Num. 15:30-31; Deut. 21:18-21). At the same time it should be noted that many felonies that today are punishable by imprisonment were, under the Mosaic Law, punishable only by fines.

Though the principle of restraint has often been advanced as an argument for the value of incarceration, mounting evidence indicates that the argument is weak. Mitford claims that "even the toughest wardens . . . agree that 75 to 90 percent of the prison population could safely be released tomorrow."[28] In the late 1960s the California legislature's Office of Research conducted some careful evaluations of the state's Department of Corrections programs. Among their findings were the following:

> The likelihood of a citizen being subjected to personal injury or property loss can be only infinitesimally lessened by the field of corrections. The increase in public protection gained by the imprisonment of large numbers of offenders, of whom few are dangerous, is outweighed by the public costs involved.[29]

Because of such evidence, many penologists are now urging that none except the especially dangerous criminal offenders be incarcerated. This exception for the especially dangerous is necessary, of course, only because capital punishment is rejected.

REHABILITATION

Rehabilitation, the transformation of criminals so that they will commit no more crimes, is today's most prominent penological objective.[30] DeFord speaks to this point.

The shift from theories of revenge, retribution, expiation, and deterrence to a theory of reformation of the offender, with its ultimate aim the protection of society, is the hallmark of today's enlightened penology. It is a necessary change-over from the old psychology of free will and deliberate preference of evil, to the modern psychology of man as a complex of influences affecting his rehabilitative programs.[31]

DeFord further maintains that any criminal, except perhaps a congenital psychopath, "can under proper treatment be reconverted into a normal social being."[32]

However, the evidence does not support this claim. Ward begins his devastating overview of evaluative studies of modern rehabilitative programs by announcing that "the claim that offenders could be 'rehabilitated' in prison has been exposed as a myth."[33]

Moreover, another of the findings of the previously cited study by the California legislature's Office of Research was that "there is no evidence to support claims that one correctional program has more rehabilitative effectiveness than another."[34] Along the same lines, Ward quotes sociologist Robert Martinson's conclusion following a critical survey of all studies of any rehabilitative program published between 1945 and 1967. Martinson concluded that "there is very little evidence in these studies that any prevailing mode of correctional treatment has a decisive effect in reducing the recidivism of convicted offenders."[35]

In light of this, the fact that there are no laws in the Mosaic code aimed directly at rehabilitating convicted offenders is not surprising. God holds people responsible for their moral choices, and the whole tenor of Scripture runs counter to the assertion that most men are reformable. Yet while the law made no explicit commitment to rehabilitation, it did contain some implicit rehabilitative elements.

First, the law indirectly rehabilitated by keeping offenders out of prison and in the community. The convicted were not subjected to all the corrupting and dehumanizing influences that are so common in prisons today,[36] simply because there were no prisons. The cities of refuge (Num. 35:9-25, 32; Deut. 19:1-10) were the nearest things to prisons. They were like prisons in that the unintentional killer was confined there, but they were unlike prisons in that their society was criminal neither in membership nor in value system.

Daniel Glaser observes,

> The most effective controls for keeping all of us conforming to the law may well be the informal social influences of home, job, and other group settings. The concern of people with their obligations to specific individuals and with their reputations among persons whose good will they value seems to regulate their behavior much more than do the formal threats, restrictions, or surveillance of government agencies.[37]

The goal of any rehabilitation program should be the reintegration of the offender into the community. Research indicates that the few favorable changes which do occur in prisons are rarely translated to the community.[38] On the other hand, some studies support the claim that offenders can be rehabilitated more completely, more inexpensively, and more quickly in the community than in prison.[39] Such evidence leads Glaser to formulate a general maxim: "Never set apart from the community, any more than can possibly be avoided, those whom you wish someday to bring safely back into the community."[40]

Second, the law was also indirectly rehabilitative in that its penalties were relevant to their corresponding crimes. Galtung notes that imprisonment has an air of irrelevancy, an irrelevancy well expressed by inmates who say that though they agree that crime should be punished, they cannot see what their imprisonment has to do with their crimes.[41] Galtung goes on to argue, in light of the irrelevance of incarceration as a punishment to its corresponding crime, that "simple pedagogical principles about the importance of uniting learning methods with learning ends can be used to predict that any case of social learning (resocialization) occurring within prison walls will be almost miraculous."[42]

In contrast, the Mosaic Law closely connected learning methods with learning ends. Its penalties were characterized by a high degree of relevance. Theft or destruction of property was punished by a fine, but not a fine paid to the government. Rather, the fine was paid to the victim as restitution for his loss. The crime of mutilation was punished by mutilation. One who perjured maliciously received the same punishment that he intended for the accused (Deut. 19:16-19). The man who socially disgraced his wife by falsely accusing her of not having been a virgin when he married her was forbidden ever to divorce her (Deut. 22:13-19), a prohibition which guaranteed her a measure of the social security she lost by the defamation. Likewise, a man who seduced or raped an unengaged virgin had to marry her if her father so desired, had to pay her father a dowry whether he married her or not, and could never divorce her (Ex. 22:16-17; Deut. 22:25-29). The man who lessened his deceased sonless brother's reputation by refusing to raise up sons to him received a punishment designed to lessen his own reputation (Deut. 25:5-10).

Third, the law indirectly rehabilitated the offender by legislating a society in which temptation to commit crime was reduced to a minimum. The Mosaic code included laws to protect the poor (Ex. 22:22-27; 23:6; Lev. 19:13; Deut. 24:12-15), to lessen the pains of their poverty (Ex. 23:11; Lev. 19:9-10; 23:22; 25:35-37; Deut. 14:25-29; 15:7-11; 23:24-25; 24:19-21; 26:12), and to prevent it from becoming permanent (Lev. 25:8-34; Num. 27:8-11; Deut. 15:1-3; 19:14). The law, anticipating that some Israelites would have to sell themselves into slavery to pay debts, contained legislation to make their slavery tolerable (Ex. 21:26-27; Lev. 25:39-43, 53), to bring it to an end (Ex. 21:2-3; Lev. 25:39-42, 47-54; Deut. 15:12), and to give them a good start following their emancipation (Deut. 15:13-14). Likewise, there were laws to protect the physically handicapped (Lev. 19:14) and the stranger (Ex.

22:21; Lev. 19:10, 33-34; 23:22; Deut. 14:29; 16:11, 14; 24:19-21; 26:12). Justice was commanded both in the market (Lev. 19:35-36; Deut. 25:13-15) and in the courts (Ex. 23:6-8; Deut. 1:16-17; 16:15-20).

It is only recently that penologists have begun to realize the importance of societal conditions for rehabilitation. Rehabilitative efforts have been psychologically oriented, concentrating almost entirely on changing the offender. Now there is beginning to emerge a new and yet untested correctional philosophy described by Flynn in terms of two main precepts:

> The first precept is that society, in addition to human attitudes, needs changing. Secondly, more emphasis should be placed on the offender's social and cultural milieu if we are to obtain any substantial relief from recidivism . . . Successful adjustment, therefore, will require personal reformation and conditions within the community that are conducive to an offender's reintegration into it.[43]

RESTITUTION

Two other penological objectives were manifested in God's law given through Moses, neither one of which is in contemporary penology. One of these was the restitution to the victim by the offender of what was lost or stolen. This objective is amply illustrated not only in the numerous fines described in Exodus 21:18-22:17 but also in the previously mentioned penalties for defaming one's wife and for violating an unengaged virgin.

Although there is an increase in court orders stipulating that restitution be made, criminals today are still infrequently held responsible to restore deprived values to victims.[44] This current penological omission often leaves the victim with a loss, and it also may lead to an unfortunate error in the criminal's thinking. Since he interacts in the penal process almost entirely with the state, he may forget that there is a victim to whom he has caused a loss, and thus he may come to view himself only as a loser in a conflict with society.[45]

PURIFICATION

The other penological purpose manifested in the Mosaic Law but not considered in modern penology is purification. Penalties, especially capital punishment, were to be administered to remove evil from the midst of Israel (Lev. 20:14; Deut. 13:5; 17:7, 12; 19:19; 21:21; 22:21-22, 24; 24:7). The point seems to have been that a crime committed within Israel constituted a polluting evil within the nation, an evil from whose guilt the nation could be cleansed only by properly punishing the offender (Num. 35:31-34; Deut. 19:13). The complete absence of such a concept in modern penology, accompanied by a shying away from severe penalties, causes one to wonder how polluted with guilt the United States must appear to God.

SOME TENTATIVE CONCLUSIONS

What suggestions for modern penology can be gleaned from a study of penological objectives in the Mosaic Law? The following proposals are offered tentatively with the suspicion that not all that was good for ancient theocratic Israel is necessarily good for modern pluralistic society.

The present prison system should be dismantled and be replaced by punishments that are more relevant, severe, and public, but less corrupting and expensive. These punishments should be primarily fiscal or physical. The process of justice should be made swifter and less benevolent to those convicted of crimes. The appeals process should be streamlined and the rights of the accused should not be exaggerated to such a degree that justice is not realized.

The concepts of justice and moral responsibility should occupy a central place in penological thinking. More emphasis should be placed on retribution and on deterrence by punishment and less on rehabilitation. Realistic rehabilitation goals should be sought less by psychological means and more by penal and sociological ones. The objective of restraint should be eliminated; the protection of the community from dangerous or habitual criminals should be secured through the reinstitution and more frequent application of capital punishment. The plight of the victim should be given more attention by including restitution as a penological objective. Likewise, more than a verbal nod should be given to God by adding the objective of national purification.

NOTES

1. David A. Ward, "Evaluative Research for Corrections," in *Prisoners in America*, ed. Lloyd E. Ohlin (Englewood Cliffs, N.J.: Prentice Hall, 1973), 184.

2. Elizabeth W. Vorenberg and James Vorenberg, "Early Diversion from the Criminal Justice System: Practice in Search of a Theory," in *Prisoners in America*, 182.

3. For a list of eight of the most basic contradictions between punishment orientation and treatment orientation see John Galtung, "Prison: The Organization of Dilemma," in *The Prison: Studies in Institutional Organization and Change*, ed. Donald R. Cressey (New York: Holt, Rinehart & Winston, 1961), 122–23. Galtung believes that the two can be combined successfully in one institution, but his proposal for doing so is not convincing.

4. References to "modern penology" in this article actually mean "modern U.S. penology." Such penology is fairly representative of that practiced in many countries, but not all (e.g., Iron Curtain countries).

5. For the sake of convenience the expression "Mosaic Law" is often used in this article, but it should always be remembered that the formulator of this legal code was not the man Moses but God himself.

6. Miriam Allen DeFord, *Stone Walls: Prisons from Fetters to Furloughs* (New York: Chilton Co., 1962), 209.

7. Edith Elisabeth Flynn, "Jails and Criminal Justice," in *Prisoners in America*, 52.

8. DeFord, *Stone Walls*, 110.

THE PURPOSE OF PENOLOGY IN THE MOSAIC LAW

9. Lloyd E. Ohlin, "Introduction," in *Prisoners in America*, 1.
10. DeFord, *Stone Walls*, 208.
11. Ibid., 209.
12. Flynn, "Jails and Criminal Justice," 53.
13. Erving Goffman, "On the Characteristics of Total Institutions: The Inmate World," in *The Prison: Studies in Institutional Organization and Change*, 66–67.
14. The number of offenses requiring the death penalty were too numerous to specify here. They included, among others, sexual immorality, disrespect for parents, kidnapping, murder, false or incorrect worship, working on the Sabbath, blaspheming God's name, failure to observe the Passover, contempt of court, perjury, and carelessness leading to the death of another. A concordance study of the expressions "put to death," "cut off," and "die" will yield almost all the capital punishment passages in the Law. The offenses can be grouped under four headings: religious error or failure, assault, sexual immorality, and stubborn or defiant disobedience to proper authority.
15. DeFord, *Stone Walls*, 2.
16. *Laws of Hammurabi*, 218.
17. C.F. Keil and Franz Delitsch, *The Pentateuch, Roman Biblical Commentary on the Old Testament*, trans. James Martin, 3 vols. (Grand Rapids: Wm. B. Eerdmans Publishing Co., 1951), 3:205.
18. K.A. Kitchen, *Ancient Orient and Old Testament* (Chicago: InterVarsity Press, 1966), 148. Also see Shalom M. Paul, *Studies in the Book of the Covenant in the Light of Cuneiform and Biblical Law*, vol. 18 of Supplements to Vetus Testamentum, (Leiden: E.J. Brill, 1970), 39.
19. Flynn, "Jails and Criminal Justice," 58.
20. Ibid.
21. "So, Give her the Money," *Newsweek*, 14 January 1974, 50–51.
22. Truman Capote, *In Cold Blood* (New York: Random House, 1965), 330.
23. Ibid.
24. Ibid.
25. Flynn, "Jails and Criminal Justice," 53.
26. DeFord, *Stone Walls*, 208–9.
27. Ibid., 183.
28. Peter S. Prescott, "In Stir," *Newsweek*, 17 September 1973, 98.
29. Ward, "Evaluative Research," 196.
30. Flynn, "Jails and Criminal Justice," 53.
31. DeFord, *Stone Walls*, 110.

32. Ibid., 219.
33. Ward, "Evaluative Research," 184.
34. Ibid., 195.
35. Ibid., 197.
36. For a summary of some of the damaging effects of prison life see Donald R. Cressey, "Adult Felons in Prison," in *Prisoners in America*, 117–19; DeFord, *Stone Walls*, 129–30; LaMar T. Empey, "Juvenile Justice Reform: Diversion, Due Process, and Deinstitutionalization," in *Prisoners in America*, 35; Donald L. Garrity, "The Prison as a Rehabilitation Agency," in *The Prison: Studies in Institutional Organization and Change*, 359; Goffman, "The Inmate World," 62–63.
37. Daniel Glaser, "Correction of Adult Offenders in the Community," in *Prisoners in America*, 97–98.
38. Flynn, "Jails and Criminal Justice," 53.
39. Empey, "Juvenile Justice Reform," 37–48; Ward, "Evaluative Research," 199–201.
40. Glaser, "Correction of Adult Offenders in the Community," 116.
41. Galtung, "Prison: The Organization of Dilemma," 107–8.
42. Ibid., 110.
43. Flynn, "Jails and Criminal Justice," 53–54.
44. Galtung, "Prison: The Organization of Dilemma," 109.
45. Ibid., 111.

10

THE DOCTRINE OF CAPITAL PUNISHMENT
Charles C. Ryrie

apital punishment, like so many controversial subjects, has ramifications in many fields. Its implications reach into the fields of penology, sociology, law, justice, but, above all, theology. Anything that touches life and death is, after all, theological, and any meaningful discussion must be so oriented. Indeed, one's theological viewpoint (or, more broadly, his philosophical orientation) will slant, if not settle, his attitude toward such a matter as capital punishment.

Capital punishment is defined as "the death penalty for crime." This includes the ideas that a crime has been committed and thus the person being executed is guilty. It also assumes that the government that carries out the sentence has been duly constituted (though the form of that government may vary). The specific crimes to which capital punishment applies cannot be stated in a definition, for this is really a separate question. The only matter to be considered is whether the principle of capital punishment is authorized by the Scriptures.

THE CURRENT DEBATE

The arguments advanced today against the legitimacy of capital punishment are usually along these lines: *Capital punishment cannot be harmonized with the love of God. The Christian gospel seeks the redemption of evildoers which is the exact opposite of all that is involved in capital punishment. Jesus "always recommended life and forgiveness over death and condemnation."*[1] This view is an outworking of liberal theology which conveniently ignores Jesus' teaching about condemnation (Matt. 5:21-26; 10:28; 12:32). It is often related to a societal redemption, rather than an individual redemption. However, evangelicals are also sometimes opposed to capital punishment, though often for reasons unrelated to theology, such as the alleged impossibility of administering the matter fairly.[2]

Humanitarianism and the dignity and worth of society are other bases for decrying capital punishment. Albert Camus asks for sympathy to be shown for the family of the victim of capital punishment, stating that the death penalty strikes at the innocent (i.e., the family of the criminal). Ramsay Clark while Deputy Attorney General stated that "this nation is so great in its resources and too good in its purposes to engage in the light of recent understanding in the deliberate taking of human life as either a punishment or a deterrent to domestic crime."[3] Coupled with these arguments is the continuous debate on the question of whether capital punishment is a deterrent to crime.[4]

Perhaps the arguments against capital punishment (especially in a religious context) are best summarized in a resolution adopted in 1960 by the American Baptist Convention. It said:

> Because the Christian believes in the inherent worth of human personality and in the unceasing availability of God's mercy, forgiveness, and redemptive power, and
>
> Because the Christian wholeheartedly supports the emphasis in modern penology upon the process of creative, redemptive rehabilitation rather than on punishment and primitive retribution, and
>
> Because the deterrent effects of capital punishment are

not supported by available evidence, and

Because the death penalty tends to brutalize the human spirit and the society which condones it, and

Because human agencies of legal justice are fallible, permitting the possibility of the executing of the innocent,

We, therefore, recommend the abolition of capital punishment and the re-evaluation of the parole system relative to such cases.[5]

On the other hand, many still argue for capital punishment. Five reasons often given are that opposition to capital punishment "sides with evil; shows more regard for the criminal than the victim of the crime; weakens justice and encourages murder; is not based on Scripture but on a vague philosophical system that makes a fetish of the idea that the taking of life is wrong, under every circumstance; and fails to distinguish adequately between killing and murder, between punishment and crime."[6]

The heart of the issue truly is, What do the Scriptures teach? One's ethics are always based on his philosophy or theology, which is ultimately related to one's view of the authority of the Bible. Though there can be honest difference of opinion between those who hold to the authority of the Bible, there can be no true light on any subject without trying to discover what the Bible says; and this is certainly true of the issue of capital punishment.

THE TEACHING OF SCRIPTURE

Genesis 9:6

That this verse established the principle of capital punishment is not debated. Murder is clearly to be punished by death

141

because of the sanctity of human life. The foundation for this drastic punishment is the fact that man was made in the image of God; therefore, when violence in the form of murder is done to a man, it is in effect an outrage against God. How punishment is to be carried out is stated to be "by man," thus leaving some flexibility as to the actual means of punishment. That the principle extends to the entire human race seems apparent from the simple fact that Noah, to whom it was given, stood at the head of a new beginning of the human race. What was given to Noah (like the permission to eat meat and the promise of no further flood) was not confined to any group or family or cult.

The Mosaic Law

The death penalty was also incorporated into the Mosaic code, with a very significant difference. Whereas Genesis 9:6 only sanctions it in cases of murder, the Mosaic code required it for other offenses. The list was as follows: murder (Ex. 21:12; Num. 35:16-31), working on the Sabbath (Ex. 35:2), cursing father or mother (Lev. 20:9), adultery (Lev. 20:10), incest (Lev. 20:11-13), sodomy (Lev. 20:13), bestiality (Lev. 20:15-16), false prophesying (Deut. 13:1-10; 18:20), idolatry (Deut. 17:2-7), incorrigible juvenile delinquency (Deut. 21:18-23), rape (Deut. 22:25), keeping an ox known to have killed a human being (Ex. 21:29), kidnapping (Ex. 21:16), and intrusion of an alien into a sacred place or office (Num. 1:51; 3:10, 38; 18:7).

John 8:1-11

Though there is a question whether this passage is a genuine part of the original text of Scripture, most scholars agree that this records a true incident in the life of Christ, and it is often used by opponents of capital punishment as indicating His abolition of it. Certain facts seem to be clear in the passage. First, the motive of the scribes and Pharisees was to tempt Christ,

142

to try to get a legal basis on which to accuse Him (v. 6). If he condoned the stoning, then He would have opened Himself to the charge of counseling action contrary to Roman law; and if He advised against stoning, He would have stood against the Mosaic Law (Lev. 20:10; Deut. 22:22). Second, the Lord's answer not only extricated Him, but raised the important point of the competency of the witnesses and accusers. If they, for instance, had not given the woman a warning, then she could not be convicted on their evidence. "No one, however factually guilty, can be lawfully convicted and executed on the evidence of incompetent witnesses. They would be 'joining with the wicked' if they allowed her, for all her adultery, to be a victim of injustice. The witnesses, and the elders, are put on their guard."[7] Third, Jesus did not reject the Mosaic Law, for He enjoined that a stone be thrown (v. 7). This is not abolition of the death penalty!

Romans 13:1-7

Several important principles are established or reaffirmed in this passage: (1) Human government is ordained by God (v. 1), yet it is a sphere of authority that is distinct from others like that of the home or the church. (2) Human government is to be obeyed by the Christian because it is of God, because it opposes evil (v. 4), and because one's conscience tells him to obey (v. 5). (3) The government has the right of taxation (vv. 6-7). (4) The government has the right to use force (v. 4), and this, of course, is the principle which impinges on the subject of capital punishment. The question is, What is included in the government's right to "bear the sword"?

Some understand that the sword does not mean the authority of government to practice capital punishment. They negate that authority on the basis of phrases which precede and follow in the context, such as "recompense to no man evil for evil," "avenge not yourselves," and "love worketh no ill to his neighbor."[8] The exegetical difficulty with doing this is simply that it fails to recognize that these exhortations are directed to the individual in relation to his responsibility to other individuals within the body of Christ, while the teaching concerning the government's bearing the sword is in an entirely different context of group action and responsibility.

Others feel that the sword does not necessarily include capital punishment in its representation. It may, for instance, simply mean a policeman's pistol, and though it means that a governmental officer can bear arms, a court probably has no right to pass the death penalty.[9]

Others unhesitatingly state that "the sword is the symbol of the magistrate's power to put to death."[10] While it is true that "the sword" may also include other rightful restraints in the proper function of government (like fines, imprisonment, confiscation of property), it clearly includes execution of the death penalty. The word *sword* is significant, for the Greek term

> denotes (in opposition to . . . the poniard or straight-edged sword) a large knife with bent blade, like that carried by the chiefs in the *Iliad,* and with which they cut the neck of the victims, similar to our sabre. Paul by this expression does not here denote the weapon which the emperor and his pretorian prefect carried as a sign of their power of life and death—the application would be too restricted—but that which was worn at their side, in the provinces, by the superior magistrates, to whom belonged the right of capital punishment, and which they caused to be borne solemnly before them in public processions.[11]

This scholar goes on to point out, as have others, that it is impossible to exclude from the right of punishing the kind of punishment which the emblem (the sword) represents. If this verse only teaches the right of capital punishment without the practice of it, then presumably taxation, mentioned in the following verses, is only a symbol of the authority and does not refer to the actual taking of money from people. That, of course, is an impossible interpretation. Likewise, it is inconceivable to consider this verse as teaching only the government's right to use capital punishment without the actual exercise of that right.

In summary, it may be said that Romans 13:4 does teach the right of government to take the life of a criminal, though in what cases is not specified. The only possible modification of the use of this principle cannot be on the basis that it is unscriptural or unchristian but unnecessary if the government can fulfill by other means its God-appointed mandate to be a terror to evildoers and an executor of wrath on those who do evil (which is quite debatable).[12] But the prerogative of capital punishment, established in Genesis 9:6, elaborated in the Mosaic code, not done away with in the teaching of Jesus, is affirmed in the doctrinal portion of the New Testament.

SOME QUESTIONS

A Biblical Question

Does the sixth commandment, "Thou shalt not kill" (Ex. 20:13, KJV) abrogate the principle of capital punishment? The verb used in this verse occurs 49 times in the Old Testament and in every relevant use means "to murder," especially with premeditation. It is never used of animals, God, angels, or enemies in battle.[13] The New Testament always translates the sixth commandment with a Greek word which is never used in any other sense than "to murder." The penalty for breaking the commandment was death (Ex. 21:12; Num. 35:16-21).

One can conclude that when the theocracy took the life of a murderer (i.e., one who violated this sixth commandment), the state (and particularly those who actually performed the execution) was not guilty of murder. Furthermore, God's commanding Israel to kill her enemies during the conquest of Canaan could not have been a violation of this commandment either by God or by the individual soldiers who killed in battle. They were the instruments of the execution of divine judg-

145

ment and not violators of the sixth commandment.[14]

A Theological Question

Does an approach to the Scriptures that sees a progress of revelation or dispensational distinctions forbid the use of Genesis 9:6 as a guideline for today? There are only two ways the answer could be yes. One is if in the progress of revelation the New Testament declared a new ethic which would replace the Old Testament ethic concerning capital punishment. But it was already seen that neither the Lord nor the apostles introduced a replacement ethic for capital punishment; indeed, they did not disturb the Old Testament standard concerning this matter (John 8:1-11; Rom. 13:1-7).

The other way would be to understand that the ending of the law in the New Testament carried with it the end of capital punishment which was an integral part of the law. Dispensationalists insist that the law has been done away with in Christ. This of course would mean that the capital punishment that was part of the Mosaic Law was superseded by the law of grace. But by no stretch of the imagination could this include Genesis 9:6. Dispensational distinctions do recognize that the law of capital punishment for certain crimes was done away with in Christ, but this does not include capital punishment for murder. If the New Testament gave a replacement for the standard of Genesis 9:6, then it would no longer be valid. But since it does not, then the dispensational teaching on the end of the Law is irrelevant to Genesis 9:6, and the principle of that verse still applies today.

A Practical Question

What, after all, is the purpose of capital punishment? Numerous answers have been given and debated, but ultimately the biblical purpose seems to be the promotion of justice by civil government. It is the purpose of government to punish those who do evil, and capital punishment is evidently one of the ways this purpose is to be promoted. This raises the question of whether or not capital punishment is really a deterrent to crime. Great Britain's experience indicates that it is: "There has been a sharp rise in armed robberies and violent crime throughout Britain since 1965, when the death penalty was dropped, and more criminals seem to carry guns now."[15] J. Edgar Hoover had an experienced appraisal: "The professional law enforcement officer is convinced from experience that the hardened criminal has been and is deterred from killing based on the prospect of the death penalty."[16] In the view of many experts, at least, capital punishment does serve a purpose which is necessary to government carrying out its God-ordained function. Without it the sword of government would be sheathed.

NOTES

1. John W. Sloat, "Let's Abolish Capital Punishment," *Pulpit Digest,* January 1970, 46.
2. "After Capital Punishment, What?" *United Evangelical Action,* May 1965, 17.
3. For these and other statements like them, see Gerald H. Gottlieb, "Capital Punishment" *Crime and Delinquency* 15 (January 1970): 2–11.
4. See *The Death Penalty in America,* ed. Hugo Adam Bedau (Garden City, N.Y.: 1964), especially chapter 6.
5. Cited in "The Argument against the Death Penalty," in *The Death Penalty in America,* 167–68.
6. Jacob J. Vellenga, "Is Capital Punishment Wrong?" *Christianity Today,* 12 October 1959, 7.
7. J. Dundan M. Derrett, *Law in the New Testament* (London: Darton, Longman, and Todd, 1970), 183.
8. Charles S. Milligan, "A Protestant's View of the Death Penalty," in *The Death Penalty in America,* 178.
9. Dwight Ericsson, "The New Testament Christianity and the Morality of Capital Punishment," *Journal of the American Scientific Affiliation* 15 (September 1962): 77–79. See also the weak interpretive paraphrase of The Living Bible at Romans 13:4: "The policeman is sent by God to help you."

10. William G.T. Shedd, *A Critical and Doctrinal Commentary Upon the Epistle of St. Paul to the Romans* (New York: 1879), 328.

11. F. Godet, *Commentary of St. Paul's Epistle to the Romans,* trans. by A. Cusin (Edinburgh: 1881), 2:311.

12. See W. Sanday, "The Epistle to the Romans," in *A Bible Commentary for Bible Students,* ed. Charles John Ellicott (London: n.d.), 7:256.

13. Of the 49 occurrences 36 are in the Pentateuch and Joshua and are related to laws regarding murder and manslaughter. Of the remaining 13, 2 involve an abstract use in the nominal form (Ps. 42:19; Ezek. 21:22), 2 are quotations of the command (Jer. 7:9; Hos. 4:2), and the 9 mean murder.

14. The commandment is without an object and thus includes a prohibition against taking one's own life.

15. Felix Kessler, "The Gun," *The Wall Street Journal,* 6 June 1972, 1.

16. J. Edgar Hoover, "Statements in Favor of the Death Penalty," *The Death Penalty in America,* 134.

11

A DISPENSATIONAL PREMILLENNIAL VIEW OF LAW AND GOVERNMENT
Norman L. Geisler

vangelical Christians differ on their views of how the
present kingdom of God relates to the future kingdom.
Their views affect their beliefs about Christian involvement in the political arena more than their ecclesiastical tradition does.

The widest difference of opinion on the relationship of the
present and future kingdoms is between the premillennial and
postmillennial views. Postmillenarians believe that the church
is obligated to usher in the kingdom. They believe that the
future kingdom (millennium) "is to be brought about by forces
now active in the world."[1] This is much different from premillenarians, who hold to a discontinuity between the present
kingdom and the future kingdom (which only Christ will personally inaugarate). Amillenarians fall somewhere in between,
though on the crucial point of whether there is continuity between the present and the future kingdom, amillenarians most
often side with the premillenarians in answering no.

HISTORY OF THE PREMILLENNIAL VIEW

The historical roots of premillennialism go back to the first
century. "Among earlier writers the belief was held by the
authors of the Epistle of Barnabas [4, 15], the Shepherd, the

149

Second Epistle of Clement, by Papias, Justin, and by some of the Ebionites, and Cerinthus."² The premillennial view was also shared by such church leaders as Irenaeus, Melito, Hippolytus, Tertullian, and Lactantius.

Eusebius recorded the millennial beliefs of Cerinthus, saying that he believed that "after the resurrection there would be an earthly kingdom of Christ."³ Of Papias, Eusebius wrote, "He says there would be a certain millennium after the resurrection and that there would be a corporeal reign of Christ on this very earth."⁴ Justin Martyr declared, "I and others, who are right-minded Christians on all points, are assured that there will be a resurrection of the dead, and a thousand years in Jerusalem, which will then be built, adorned, and enlarged, [as] the prophets Ezekiel and Isaiah and others declare."⁵ Tertullian wrote, "We confess that a kingdom is promised to us upon earth, only in another state of existence; inasmuch as it will be after the resurrection for a thousand years in the divinely built city of Jerusalem."⁶

The premillennial view continued strong until the fourth century, when it was at first embraced by Augustine. However, he later gave it up, though he never undertook to refute it. He even conceded that it would not be objectionable as long as the premillenarians did not "assert that those who then rise again shall enjoy the leisure of immoderate carnal banquets."⁷

Augustine's reaction to premillennialism prevailed in medieval Roman Catholicism up to the Reformation, in which the primary concern was with the doctrine of salvation and not "the last things." However, even during the Reformation the premillennial view was strongly represented by the Swiss brethren such as Conrad, Grebel, Felix Manz, and George Blaurock. The Dutch Anabaptist Meno Simmons was also premillennial. The German Calvinist Johann Heinrich Alsted returned to the premillennial view of the early church fathers in his book *The Beloved City*, which caused the learned Anglican scholar Joseph Mede to become a premillenarian. In America the millennial position was forwarded by Cotton Mather, who held that "there will be a time when Jerusalem shall be literally rebuilt, and people all over the world shall be under the influence of that Holy City."[8] John Edwards believed in six dispensations and a thousand-year reign of Christ, albeit a spiritual one.

Crucial for this study is Isaac Watts (1674–1748), who was not only premillennial but also a forerunner of dispensationalism. He outlined six dispensations plus a millennium which correspond exactly to those given later in the Scofield Bible.[9] He also referred to a dispensational view of civil government. Johann H. Bengel, Isaac Newton, and Joseph Priestly carried on the dispensational or premillennial view in the 18th century. In the 19th century Edward Irving of the Church of Scotland fostered a widespread interest in premillennialism. The latter part of the 19th century witnessed a full-blown form of dispensational premillennialism in the writings of John Nelson Darby.[10]

At the turn of the century, C.I. Scofield, through his enormously popular reference Bible, had a wide influence on American premillennialism. And through Lewis Sperry Chafer and Dallas Theological Seminary (established in 1924), dispensational premillennialism has spread throughout the world.

Premillennialism dominates a broad section of American theological schools, many of which are dispensational as well. To say the least, the premillennial view has an early and venerable history and is perhaps the dominant evangelical view in the United States today. It is important then to note how premillenarianism, in contrast to postmillenarianism, affects one's view toward law and government.

THE POSTMILLENNIAL POSITION

Though the early American tradition was largely dominated by postmillenarians, relatively few evangelicals today hold that view. Hence it is a misdirection for contemporary premillenarians (and amillenarians) to call America back to its so-called Christian foundations. For whatever Christian influence there was in early America was largely postmillennial, not premillennial (or amillennial).

In fact, today not a single evangelical seminary is committed to postmillenarianism. The strongest postmillennial influence in America today comes from the small group of Chalcedon theonomists, such as Greg Bahnsen, Gary North, and others, who believe that Christians are obligated to set up a Christian government in America. As Rushdoony put it, "The saints must prepare to take over the world's government and its courts."[11]

Rushdoony opposes democracy, saying, "Democracy requires identification with the continuum, and such identification necessitates a surrender of all exclusive and aristocratic concepts."[12] He believes that democracy is opposed to Christianity, insisting that "the choice, ultimately, is the basic one between democracy and traditional Christian theology."[13] More than this, "Supernatural Christianity is basically and radically antidemocratic."[14] Indeed, Rushdoony believes, "democracy is the great love of the failures and cowards of life, and involves a hatred of differences."[15]

Rushdoony is equally opposed to equality, saying, "The only conclusion of such a course of action is bankruptcy, both moral and financial bankruptcy, because the very idea of law is against equality." In fact, "equality is a high sounding but impossible dream."[16] Rushdoony actually favors a kind of caste system, contending that "no society has ever existed without class and castelines."[17]

Bahnsen carries through consistently Rushdoony's idea of theonomy and concludes that Christians should still practice the Old Testament law today, including capital punishment for kidnappers, homosexuals, and rebellious children. He concludes "that there is a continuity between the law of God in the Older Testament and New Testament morality: Christ has confirmed every jot and tittle of the law."[18] This means that the state must be based on the Bible. For "the doctrine of the state presented by Paul in Romans 13 is a reaffirmation of the essential Older Testament conception of the civil magistrate."[19]

A DISPENSATIONAL PREMILLENNIAL VIEW OF LAW

While most amillenarians disavow the extremes of postmillennialism, some have come close to seeking to set up their own kingdom. Calvin's Geneva is a case in point. The Roman Catholic Church, holding an amillennial Augustinian view, has also manifested this propensity from Constantine to this century. However, unlike the postmillennial view, nothing inherent in amillenarianism demands that Christians politically prepare for the setting up of Christ's kingdom. On the contrary, most amillenarians look to the future return of Christ and to His eternal reign as discontinuous with the present.[20] Hence they do not view their present social involvement as directly related to the emergence of the future kingdom of God. In this respect, amillenarians are more like premillenarians.

THE PREMILLENNIAL POSITION

Some premillenarians have gone to an opposite extreme from postmillenarians on social and political issues. Some have urged believers not to polish the brass rails on the sinking social ship. Rather, they urge Christians to be engaged in "saving souls." A famous contemporary premillennial evangelist quips that he has no time to clean up the cesspool because he is too busy fishing (for souls) in it. Early this century I.M. Haldeman insisted that "trying to save the world by socialism was like cleaning and decorating the staterooms of a sinking ship."[21]

Many premillenarians, however, have been deeply involved in social matters. Timothy Smith has written of the important role of premillennial thought in social renewal.[22] This was true of earlier fundamentalists and evangelicals, as well as contemporary ones. A.C. Dixon, editor of *The Fundamentals* (1910-1915), even went so far as to encourage Christians to organize political parties "for the carrying forward of any great reform."[23] James Gray, a former president of Moody Bible Institute, and William Riley, an influential Baptist pastor from Minneapolis, both had strong social emphases in the early 20th century, as did A.J. Gordon of Boston. Wheaton College has also had a strong premillennial influence in social and cultural areas. Much of the strongest influence for Christian social involvement in contemporary America has been and is being generated by premillennial leaders such as Jerry Falwell, Timothy LaHaye, Pat Robertson, and Francis Schaeffer.

What is of interest here is to explore the genius of premillennialism, especially as it relates to law and government. To do this, attention is drawn to the early roots of the modern premillennial movement, especialy to some of the dispensationalists. Several characteristic features of premillennial dispensationalism enabled it to form a moderating view between noninvolvement on the one hand and setting up a kind of theocracy or theonomy on the other.

The Belief That Only Christ's Return Will Bring in the Kingdom

Premillennialists believe that there will be no true theocracy until Christ returns to earth. Hence they are relieved of the unnecessary and heavy burden postmillenarians have placed on themselves to bring in the kingdom. Postmillennial optimism overlooks the depravity of man. To bring in the kingdom of God, postmillenarians realize they must Christianize the world and believe that eventually "evil in all its many forms will be reduced to negligible proportions" and "the race, as a race, will be saved."[24] The scholar B.B. Warfield expressed this optimism when he wrote, "It is solely by reasoning that [Christianity] has come thus far on its way to its kingship. And it is solely by reasoning that it will put all its enemies under its feet."[25]

The early 20th-century Scottish theologian, James Orr, also believed in the development of the race to the point of millennial perfection.[26] This is why, contrary to what one might expect, the early fundamentalists were favorable to Darwinism, while the liberals opposed it.[27] They saw natural selection as a divinely appointed natural means for the biological and social evolution of the race. American political aspirations for the "New Deal," the "Great Society," and the like were also supported.

Premillenarians, on the other hand, do not believe the millennium will come about by any political process continuous with the present. They insist rather on a divine, cataclysmic, and supernatural inauguration of the reign of Christ on earth. This relieves premillennialists of any divine duty to Christianize the world. Their duty is to be salt, content with a democracy or any government which allows freedom to preach the gospel. They are to evangelize all people (Matt. 28:18-20). Their obligation is not to bring all men to Christ, but to bring Christ to all men.

The Belief in Religious Pluralism

Premillenarians, unlike postmillenarians, do not attempt to set up a distinctly Christian government; they work rather for good government. Premillenarians need not work for Christian civil laws but only for fair ones. Their effort is not to achieve religious superiority for Christianity but religious equality before the law for all religions. In short, the premillennial position is compatible with a true pluralism. It fits well with the First Amendment of the United States Constitution which is against the state's establishing (or preferring) one religion over another.

Postmillenarians, on the other hand, are uncomfortable with religious pluralism. They sometimes concede religious liberty to others under their Christian-dominated state, but even this has limits. In early America there was discrimination against those who chose not to be religious. Many states required belief in God (theism) as a prerequisite for public office which lingered on the law books into the 1940s. This is consistent with the postmillennial need to establish God's rule on earth.

The Ten Commandments are a case in point. Postmillennialists believe that the Ten Commandments are the basis for civil law. This, however, is impossible if true freedom of religion is to be allowed. For the first commandment(s) demands allegiance to a monotheistic God as opposed to all false gods or idols. If the civil law of the United States followed the Ten Commandments, then there would be no freedom of religion for polytheists, Taoists, Hindus, Buddhists, secular humanists, or atheists. So making the Bible the basis for civil law is a contradiction to freedom of religion which exists in the United States today. But if the Bible is not the basis for civil law, what is? This leads to the next characteristic of the premillennial view.

The View That God's Revelation in Nature Is the Basis for Civil Government

While premillenarians, especially dispensationalists, do not believe that Christians are living under the Old Testament Law today, this in no way means they are against law. To be sure, dispensational premillenarians insist that the Old Testament Law was given only to the Jews and not to Gentiles.[28] And they argue that the Old Testament Law has been done away by Christ. However, most premillenarians recognize that God has not left Himself without a witness in that He has revealed a moral law in the hearts and consciences of all men (Rom. 2:14-15).

Isaac Watts, an early dispensationalist, is exemplary of this position. Building on the natural law ethic of Richard Hooker, an Anglican who followed Thomas Aquinas, Watts argued that "the design of civil government is to secure the persons, the properties, the just liberty, and peace of mankind from the invasions and injuries of their neighbors."[29] Further, neither "the things of religion, nor the affairs of a future state, come within its cognizance."[30] Nevertheless, "civil government is an ordinance of God, and appointed by Him according to the light of reason. Thus government itself is a necessary thing in this world, and a natural moral institution of God among persons of all sorts of religion, whether heathen, Turks, or Christians to preserve them in perfect peace."[31] According to Watts, government should not alter any of these religions, "nor do any of these religions alter the nature of civil government."[32]

Government is not based on special revelation, the Bible. It is based on God's general revelation to all people. Watts followed John Locke in "showing that the Jewish government was a theocracy wherein God, even Jehovah, the one true God, was their political king, and therefore the acknowledgement of any other God was treason against the state; but it was never so in any other nation upon earth."[33] Since civil law is not based on God's special revelation, it is tolerant even of idolatry.

Thus civil law, based as it is on natural moral law, lays no specifically religious obligation on people. For "every man, both governor and governed, ought to have full liberty to worship God in that special way and manner which his own conscience believes to be of divine appointment."[34] But "this is a personal obligation which natural conscience, or the light of reason, which is the candle of the Lord within us, lays on every individual person among mankind" and "peculiar religion does not break in upon the just rights or the peace of our neighbors."[35]

So "the supreme power of any state has no right to impose the profession or practice of any one peculiar religion upon the people."[36] In short, "the power of civil government reaches no further than the preservation of the natural and civil welfare, rights, and properties of mankind with regard to this world, and has nothing to do with religion further than this requires."[37] Watts is emphatic in his conclusion that "the gospel of Christ does not pretend to erect a kingdom of this world, and therefore it alters nothing in the nature of civil government (Matt. 22:21)."[38]

Based on this general revelation, man enters into social contracts in which "he engages himself with his powers and capacities to defend and preserve the peace, order, and government of the society." Indeed, "the very reason of man and the nature of things show us the necessity of such agreements."[39]

157

The civil law, however, does have a moral basis in what Watts called variously "nature," "laws of nature," "natural rights," "natural conscience," "reason," "principles of reason," "light of reason," "divine revelation," "candle of the Lord," and "ordinances of God."[40] For Watts, the natural moral law includes such things as honesty, justice, truth, gratitude, goodness, honor, and faithfulness to superiors. The laws of nature also include personal duties such as sobriety, temperance, frugality, and industry.[41] In brief, they include the kinds of things addressed in the second table of the Mosaic Law (attitudes and actions toward men) but not the first table of the Law (those toward God).

While dispensationalists' views are not all the same on this point, major contemporary proponents are in general agreement on the nature of general revelation. Chafer quoted with approval *The Scofield Reference Bible* when he wrote, "The Christian is called upon, then, to recognize [existing] human government as of God (Rom. 13:1-7; 1 Peter 2:13-17; cf. Matt. 22:21)."[42] Chafer balanced this by the recognition that "in Luke 4:5-6 it is clearly indicated that the governments of this world system (cf. Matt. 4:8-9) are under Satan's authority."[43] So the present form of the kingdom is "a mixed bag." There are good fish and bad fish, wheat and tares.

For these premillenarians the present (mystery) form of the kingdom (Matt. 13) is different from the future (messianic) form of the kingdom. Both Scofield[44] and Chafer[45] recognize that a real pluralism will exist in the present kingdom until Christ comes. Scofield wrote, "The parable of the wheat and tares is not a description of the world, but of that which professes to be the kingdom."[46] Chafer is more precise when he noted that "the kingdom of heaven is the rule of God in the earth, [and] it is now present to the extent to which He is exercising authority over the affairs of the cosmos."[47] But, he adds, "Certainly this does not depict a regenerated world. It clearly pictures an outcalled people [the church] together with the full ripening of iniquity in the unregenerate portion of humanity."[48]

According to dispensationalists, the wheat and the tares must be allowed to grow together in this present age. Religious pluralism must prevail. Only when Christ comes will He (not Christians) pluck out the wheat. Meanwhile, believers must be content to plant and cultivate wheat, not to cut down tares. This does not mean that there is no moral basis for society. Most dispensationalists recognize a general revelation for all men (Rom. 1:18-20; 2:14-15). Chafer claims that this general revelation, or "natural theology," is part of the data (along with the Bible) of systematic theology.[49] As Witmer noted, "The Law is not to be found only on tablets of stone and included in the writings of Moses; it is also inscribed in their [moral Gentiles'] hearts and is reflected in their actions, consciences, and thoughts."[50]

Because postmillenarians insist that Christians must begin to establish Christ's kingdom now before He returns, they must work to eliminate true politically encouraged religious pluralism. Herein lies the difference between premillenarians and postmillenarians in their views on government. And it has great relevance to the kind of involvement called for in the present social and political arena. Postmillenarians work to make a Christian America. Premillenarians work for a truly free America.

Combining these two features of non-theocracy (or non-theonomy) and natural law, premillennial dispensationalism makes a unique contribution to the relationship of Christians to civil government. By denying the postmillennial theocratic basis for civil government, the premillennial position avoids destroying religious freedom, and by basing civil government in the general moral law of God, it avoids destroying any moral basis for society.

A word of warning is called for here for premillenarians. It is disastrous for them to deny any general moral-law basis for civil government, as some have done.[51] For then society would be left without an ultimate moral ground and would be subject to political tyranny and social pragmatism. This is contrary to the general revelation of Romans 2:14-15 and to the command in 1 Timothy 2:2 to pray (and work) for a godly, tranquil life.

A CASE IN POINT: CIVIL DISOBEDIENCE

The premillennial view of government can be applied to the question of civil disobedience. This example will serve to differentiate a consistent premillennial view from a consistent postmillennial view on a hotly-debated contemporary issue. Many evangelicals are calling for civil disobedience, even revolution, against a government. Francis Schaeffer, for example, insisted that Christians should disobey government when "any office commands that which is contrary to the word of God."[52] He even urges a blood revolution, if necessary, against any government which makes such laws. He explains that "in a fallen world, force in some form will always be necessary."[53]

If one takes Francis Schaeffer's suggestions seriously, then all civil laws must be based on the Bible, or at least not contrary to it. But nowhere in the Bible is God's judgment of the nations based on His special written revelation (the Bible). Rather, it is always based on general principles of goodness and justice known to all men by general revelation (cf. Amos 1; Obad. 1; Jonah 3:8-10; Nahum 2). Furthermore, there was God-ordained civil government (cf. Gen. 9:6) long before there was a Bible.

What then is the essential difference between the premillenial and the postmillennial views regarding Christian obedience to government? The former can be summarized as follows.

Civil Government Is Ordained by God for All Men

According to Scripture, civil law is not based on the Christian mandate to preach the gospel to all nations (Matt. 28:18-20) but in the cultural mandate to subdue all things in creation (Gen. 1:28). This was reinforced by God ordaining the sword for capital punishment of capital crimes (Gen. 9:6). The God-ordained nature of human government is clearly spelled out in Romans 13:1-7 and 1 Peter 2:13-14. Several facts stand out in the Romans passage.

First, even oppressive governments have God-ordained authority, such as Nero's Rome which is referred to in this passage. Indeed, Nero was called a "minister of God" (Rom. 13:4).

Second, the reference in Romans 13 says that the legitimate government is the one in power. According to Romans 13:1, the "existing governments are ordained of God." Thus, Christians (and all men) are to "submit" to them (Rom. 13:1) and to "obey" them (Titus 3:1).

Third, there is no conditional clause in Romans 13 such as "obey governments only if they are just." Likewise, the command to pay taxes (Rom. 13:7) is not accompanied by any condition such as "pay taxes only if the government is using one's money for moral causes." As Princeton theologian Charles Hodge wrote, "We are to obey all that is in actual authority over us, whether their authority be legitimate or usurped, whether they are just or unjust."[54]

Disobedience Is Allowed Only When Government Usurps God's Authority

Since Romans 13:1 notes that all authority comes from God, it is assumed here (and made clear elsewhere) that human authority cannot usurp God's authority over the individual. Hence, disobedience to government becomes necessary when the government usurps the authority of God. The Scriptures include numerous examples of divinely approved disobedience to human government. The following is a complete list of circumstances when God clearly approved of believers disobeying civil law:

1. When it does not allow worship of God (Ex. 5:1).
2. When it commands believers to kill innocent people (Ex. 1:15-21).

3. When it commands that God's servants be killed
(1 Kings 18:1-4).
4. When it commands believers to worship idols (Dan.
3).
5. When it commands believers to pray only to a man
(Dan. 6).
6. When it forbids believers to propagate the gospel
(Acts 4:17-19).
7. When it commands believers to worship a man (Rev.
13).

All these cases have this in common: whereas believers are always to obey government when it takes its place under God, they should never obey it when it takes the place of God. In short, governments and laws can permit evil, but they cannot command it. For example, they can allow citizens to worship idols but they cannot insist that all do so. The authority of government ends where the conscience of the believer begins.

The Bible Places Limits on How One Can Disobey Government

There are biblical limits on how and when believers can disobey government. First, disobedience is not allowed simply because the government limits religious freedom. Rather, government must negate freedom. All laws limit freedom. It is the nature of law to draw lines so that one may know where his freedom ends and another person's begins. Thus government regulations regarding zoning, parking, and safety are not in themselves oppressive and should be obeyed, even though they limit the freedom a church has. But if the government mandates teachings or practices contrary to Scripture, the Christian should refuse to comply. That is, the government must eliminate religious freedom, not simply regulate it, before a believer should disobey the government.

Second, Christian noncompliance to oppressive laws should be a refusal, but not a revolt. That is, their disobedience should be passive, not active. They can be unsubmissive, but they must not be insubordinate. Even when a believer cannot submit to the law he must be willing to submit to the consequence of that law. Peter refused to stop preaching but he did not refuse to go to prison (Acts 5). Daniel refused to pray to the king, but he did not refuse to go to the lions' den (Dan. 6). And the three Hebrew young men would not bow, but they were willing to burn (Dan. 3). A good example of this attitude comes from the Hessian Anabaptists in the 16th century. Having been accused of sedition, their response was: "These who are not obedient to the authorities . . . should be punished with the sword by the imperial edict. We do not want to be disobedient to worldly authorities. If we have done evil, then we accept the adequate judgment."[55] This same attitude was true of many Anabaptists in the 16th and 17th centuries in Switzerland, Germany, Austria, Moravia, and the Netherlands.

To contemporize the principle, Christians should refuse to kill a human life by abortion, even if the government commands it. But they should not revolt against a government nor withhold taxes from a government which allows abortion. Of course, they may work legally to change the abortion law. But commanding Christians to have an abortion and simply permitting non-Christians to do so are two different things. Or to change the illustration, commanding a Christian to worship an idol is oppressive, but laws merely permitting others to worship idols are not oppressive and should not be overthrown.

The Israelites refused to obey Pharaoh's command, but they did not revolt against him. They followed a "love it or leave it" policy with Egypt, but they did not attack it. Rather, the sword is given to the government to use on the governed (Gen. 9:6; Rom. 13:4). The only legitimate use of the sword for citizens is to protect themselves against other citizens. Jesus said, "All who draw the sword will die by the sword" (Matt. 26:52). Revolutions in Scripture are not condoned, including Korah's, Absalom's, and Jeroboam's. The revolution of those who killed wicked Queen Athaliah and installed Joash was a special, divinely approved event in order to preserve the bloodline of the Messiah (2 Chron. 22–23). Therefore it cannot serve as a basis for other revolutions any more than the theocratic command for Israel to slaughter the Canaanites can be used to promote the genocide of a country today. In fact, the Bible forbids even associating with revolutionaries, saying, "Fear the Lord and the king, my son, and do not join with the rebellious" (Prov. 24:21). Keil and Delitzsch describe those named here as "dissidents, oppositionists, or revolutionaries."[56]

By contrast to this premillennial perspective, it is consistent with postmillenarianism to use arms to overthrow one's government if it falls short of God's demands. As a theocracy, Israel fought for God, and if the church assumes Israel's role, as postmillenarians claim it does, then it is consistent to claim that the church also assumes the use of Israel's sword. And if the sword can be used to promote the kingdom of God on earth, why should a postmillenarian, who believes he is commissioned to promote God's kingdom rule in present civil government, refuse to use the sword?

Herein lies the crucial difference between the premillennial and postmillennial perspectives on the Christian's relationship to civil government. Premillenarians can promote true religious pluralism; postmillenarians cannot. Premillenarians await Christ's coming with his armies to set up His kingdom (Rev. 19:11; 2 Thes. 1:7-9); postmillenarians do not. For the latter view themselves as the army of God to usher in Christ's kingdom here and now. This principal difference has a wide range of ramifications for contemporary conflicts between church and state.

While the premillennial view avoids a repressive theonomist perspective, it nonetheless provides a common moral basis for civil law in God's general revelation to all men. In this way, Christian social and political action (e.g., changing abortion laws), can be performed without hesitation because such is based on a common moral law revealed to all men. On the other hand, Christians should be careful to resist any attempt of government to provide a religious advantage to any one religion over another, even if it is their own.

But in the postmillennial view, the church assumes the role of Old Testament Israel, not of a distinctly new group called out of the world. Hence there is no sufficient reason why it should not set up a society like Israel's which is based on biblical principles. This same danger is inherent in the amillennial view too, since it believes that the New Testament church carries on the mission of Old Testament Israel. There is, however, one difference which saves amillennialism from the extremes of postmillennialism. An amillenarian believes that there is a future kingdom (the eternal state) which does not grow naturally out of the present one but which will be inaugurated only by Christ. It is this similarity with the premillennial view which saves them in part from the need to set up a kingdom here and now, though not all amillenarians have made this connection.

Premillennialism, in contrast to the liabilities of both postmillennialism and amillenialism, can avoid the extremes of social neglect on the one hand and of theonomy on the other hand. Thus premillennialism is uniquely capable of providing a moral basis for society (in general revelation) without denying religious freedom to any by setting up a monotheistic theonomy or biblionomy.

NOTES

1. Loraine Boettner, "Postmillennialism," in *The Meaning of the Millennium: Four Views*. ed. Robert G. Clouse (Downers Grove, Ill.: InterVarsity Press, 1977), 117.
2. J.F. Bethune-Baker, *An Introduction to the Early History of Christian Doctrine* (London: Methuen & Co., 1942), 69.
3. Eusebius Pamphilus, *The Ecclesiastical History of Eusebius Pamphilus* (Grand Rapids: Baker Book House, 1955), 113.
4. Ibid.
5. Justin Martyr, *Dialogue with Trypho,* The Ante-Nicene Fathers, ed. Alexander Roberts and James Donaldson, 9 vols. (Grand Rapids: Wm. B. Eerdmans Publishing Co., 1977) 1:239.

6. Tertullian, *Against Marcion*, The Ante-Nicene Fathers, 3:342.

7. Augustine, *City of God*, The Nicene and Post-Nicene Fathers, ed. Philp Schaff, 14 vols. (Grand Rapids: Wm. B. Eerdmans Publishing Co., 1956), 2:426.

8. Cotton Mather, *Things to Be Look'd For* (New England: n.p., 1691), 1.4.

9. Isaac Watts, *The Works of the Rev. Isaac Watts, D.D.*, 7 vols. (Leeds: Edward Baines, n.d.) 2:625.

10. John Darby, *The Collected Writings of J.N. Darby*, ed. William Kelly, 34 vols. (reprint, Sunbury, Penn.: Believers Bookshelf, 1971), 2:568–73.

11. Rousas J. Rushdoony, "Government and the Christian," *The Rutheford Institute* 1 (July–August 1984): 7.

12. Rousas J. Rushdoony, *The Messianic Character of American Education* (Phillipsburg, N.J.: Presbyterian and Reformed Publishing Co., 1963), 149.

13. Ibid., 198.

14. Ibid., 157.

15. Rousas J. Rushdoony, *Thy Kingdom Come* (Phillipsburg, N.J.: Presbyterian and Reformed Publishing Co., 1971), 39.

16. Rousas J. Rushdoony, *Bread upon the Waters* (Nutley, N.J.: Craig Press, 1969), 87.

17. Rousas J. Rushdoony, *The Foundations of Social Order* (Phillipsburg, N.J.: Presbyterian and Reformed Publishing Co., 1968), 1968.

18. Greg L. Bahnsen, *Theonomy in Christian Ethics* (Nutley, N.J.: Craig Press, 1979), 398.

19. Ibid.

20. Anthony A. Hoekema, "Amillenialism," in *The Meaning of the Millennium: Four Views*, 150.

21. I.M. Haldeman, *The Mission of the Church in the World* (New York: Book Stall, 1917), 280–87.

22. Timothy L. Smith, *Revivalism and Social Reform* (Baltimore: Johns Hopkins University Press, 1980), 257–58.

23. See George M. Marsden, *Fundamentalism and American Culture: The Shaping of Twentieth-Century Evangelicalism: 1870–1925* (Oxford: Oxford University Press, 1980), 88–89.

24. Boettner, "Postmillenialism," 118, 123.

25. Benjamin B. Warfield, "Introduction," in Francis R. Beattie, *Apologetics* (Richmond, Va.: Presbyterian Committee of Publication, n.d.), 1:26.

26. James Orr, *The Christian View of God and the Word* (Grand Rapids: Wm. B. Eerdmans Publishing Co., 1948), chap. 9.

27. James R. Moore, *The Post-Darwinian Controversies* (Cambridge: Cambridge University Press, 1979).

28. Lewis Sperry Chafer, *Systematic Theology,* 8 vols. (Dallas, Texas: Dallas Seminary Press, 1947), 4:234–43.

29. Isaac Watts, *The Works of the Rev. Isaac Watts, D.D.,* 3:325.

30. Ibid., 330.

31. Ibid.

32. Ibid.

33. Ibid., 336.

34. Ibid., 343.

35. Ibid.

36. Ibid., 356.

37. Ibid., 361.

38. Ibid.

39. Ibid., 329–30.

40. Ibid., 328–30, 334, 341, 343.

41. Ibid., 334–35.

42. Chafer, *Systematic Theology,* 7:177.

43. Ibid.

44. C.I. Scofield, *The Scofield Reference Bible* (New York: Oxford University press, 1967), 1014–15.

45. Chafer, *Systematic Theology,* 7:177.

46. Scofield, *The Scofield Reference Bible,* 1015.

47. Chafer, *Systematic Theology,* 5:352.

48. Ibid.

49. Ibid., 1:4–5.

50. John A. Witmer, "Romans," in *The Bible Knowledge Commentary,* ed. John F. Walvoord and Roy B. Zuck, 2 vols. (Wheaton, Ill.: Victor Books, 1983), 2:446.

51. J.N. Darby, *Exposition of the Epistle to the Romans* (London: N. Moorish, n.d.), 25.

52. Francis A. Schaeffer, *A Christian Manifesto* (Westchester, Ill.: Crossway Books, 1981), 90.

53. Ibid., 107.

54. Charles Hodge, *Commentary on the Epistle to the Romans* (1886; reprint, Grand Rapids: Wm. B. Eerdmans Publishing Co., 1947), 406.

55. Franz Gunther, ed., *Urkundliche Quellen zur Hessishen,* trans. Timothy Dalzell (Marburg: Waldeck, 1951), 179.

56. C.F. Keil and F. Delitzsch, "Proverbs," in *Commentary on the Old Testament in Ten Volumes* (reprint, [25 vols. in 10]; Grand Rapids: Wm. B. Eerdmans Publishing Co., 1975), 6:138.

12

THEONOMY AND DISPENSATIONALISM

Robert P. Lightner

O ne of the great issues affecting the eschatological thinking of evangelicals is the current debate concerning theonomy. Those who reject amillennialism are not only the premillennial, pretribulational dispensationalists. Postmillennialists do as well, insisting that the Mosaic Law in its entirety is just as much God's rule of life for the world today as it was in the days of Moses. They happily accept the designation "theonomists."[1]

Dispensationalists have been known more for their forthright proclamation of "thus saith the Lord," as they have understood it, than for their responses to criticism and accusations leveled against them. And yet there are times when issues challenging dispensationalism seem to demand response. I believe that theonomy is such an issue. And it is past time for dispensationalists to reply to theonomy and its postmillennial emphasis. Theonomy is a growing concern in both covenantal and dispensational circles. Kline, a committed amillennialist, for example, in his review of Greg L. Bahnsen's *Theonomy in Christian Ethics,* placed Bahnsen alongside Rousas J. Rushdoony as fellow theonomists. Kline expresses criticism of both theonomy and dispensationalism:

> Their [theonomists'] special thesis is that the Mosaic Law, more or less in its entirety, constitutes a continuing

norm for mankind and that it is the duty of the civil magistrate to enforce it, precepts and penalties alike. To put the matter in a comparative perspective, this theory of theonomic politics stands at the opposite end of the spectrum of error from dispensationalism. The latter represents an extreme of failure to do justice to the continuity between the old and new covenants. Chalcedon's [theonomy's] error, no less extreme or serious, is a failure to do justice to the discontinuity between the old and new covenants.[2]

THEONOMY

The word *theonomy* is now becoming common in theological circles. The English word comes from two Greek words for "God" and "law." Its broadest meaning therefore is "law of God." Of course Christians have always honored God's Law given through Moses. It is indeed a revelation of Himself.

But the word is now being used to designate a new idea gaining ground in some circles, particularly those emphasizing Reformed doctrine, that the governments of the world today should be guided in their judicial decisions by all the legislation of the Old Testament and, in particular, should assess the Old Testament penalties for any infraction to those laws, whether civil or religious.[3]

The most important recent contribution to theonomy is Bahnsen's *Theonomy in Christian Ethics* (Presbyterian and Reformed Publishing Company 1977, second enlarged edition, 1984). As the title indicates, Bahnsen seeks to show how "the law of God" relates to Christian behavior.

Matthew 5:17-19

One of the major chapters in *Theonomy in Christian Ethics*

169

which forms the scriptural platform for the entire work is entitled "The Abiding Validity of the Law in Exhaustive Detail (Matt. 5:17-19)." Bahnsen's view of this passage is shared by theonomists in general:

> In speaking to all those who are the sons of Abraham by faith in the Messiah (cf. Gal. 3:7), Jesus binds us to all the commandments of God forever. The poetry of the older testament also extols the eternality of the Lord's commandments. "All his precepts are trustworthy. They are established forever and ever to be performed with faithfulness and uprightness" (Ps. 111:7, RSV). "Thy testimonies are fully confirmed; holiness befits thy house, 0 Lord, forevermore" (Ps. 93:5, NASB). "All thy commandments are truth. Of old I have known from thy testimonies, that thou hast founded them forever" (Ps. 119:151-152, NASB). Indeed, every jot and tittle holds forever: "The sum of thy word is truth and every one of thy righteous ordinances is everlasting" (Ps. 119:160, NASB). The older testamental prophets confirm this truth. Although human life may be short and fragile, "the word of our God stands forever" (Isa. 40:8); Isaiah does not disqualify the prescriptions of YAHWEH (e.g., 1:10). The ethical stipulations of the covenant are part of that word for YAHWEH which endures forever. Thus the righteous law of God shall not be abolished (51:6).[4]

The theonomist interpretation of Matthew 5:17-19, which interestingly takes a rather literal view of biblical words like *all, forever,* and *everlasting,* also claims support from other rather significant sources. The following three quotations from Calvin, Warfield, and Honeyman each receive Bahnsen's full endorsement and agreement. First Calvin:

> When the Lord testifies that He "came not to abolish the law but to fulfill it" and that "until heaven and earth pass

THEONOMY AND DISPENSATIONALISM

away . . . not a jot will pass away from the law . . . "
(Matt. 5:17-18), He sufficiently confirms that by His coming nothing is going to be taken away from the observance of the law, and justly—inasmuch as He came rather to remedy transgressions of it. Therefore through
Christ the teaching of the law remains inviolable; by
teaching, admonishing, reproving, and correcting, it in-
forms us and prepares us for every good work (cf. 2 Tim.
3:16-17).[5]

Warfield's statement on the passage also meets with
Bahnsen's approval: "It is asserted with an emphasis which
could not be made stronger, that the Law in its smallest details
remains undiminished authority so long as the world lasts."[6]

Honeyman says this on the passage: "The attitude towards
the law expressed by Jesus in Matthew 5:15-20 is one of
unqualified acceptance and approval. The law is to be observed
in every detail. There is no suggestion that there is any limit in
time to its observance. The law is eternal and its most minute
prescription retains its validity . . . so long as the created
world endures, to the end of time."[7]

Church Law Society

Besides insisting that the entire Mosaic Law is operative for
believers, theonomists also hold that the church is obligated to
promote and enforce obedience to God's law in society as well.
In introducing his work, Bahnsen stated this clearly: "Hence
my present thesis is not restricted to the individual's personal
obligation to keep God's law, but I have gone on to discuss the
public obligation to promote and enforce obedience to God's
law in society as well."[8] This view is not peculiar to Bahnsen.
Chilton stated that Matthew 5:13-16 "is nothing less than a
mandate for the complete social transformation of the entire
world."[9] And he added:

The center of Christian reconstruction is the church. The

171

River of Life does not flow out from the doors of the chambers of Congresses and Parliaments. It flows from the restored Temple of the Holy Spirit, the church of Jesus Christ. Our goal is world dominion under Christ's Lordship, a *world takeover* if you will; but our strategy begins with reformation, reconstruction of the church. From that will flow social and political reconstruction, indeed a flowering of Christian civilization (Hag. 1:1-15; 2:6-9, 18-23).[10]

The Christian goal for the world is the universal development of biblical theocratic republics, in which every area of life is redeemed and placed under the Lordship of Jesus Christ and the rule of God's law.[11]

Rushdoony wrote, "The whole purpose of God's law is that covenant man assume the central task of government apart from the state and in terms of his responsibility under God."[12] His understanding of 1 Corinthians 6:2-6 ("Do you not know that the saints will judge the world? And if the world is judged by you, are you not competent to constitute the smallest law courts?") is that "the saints must prepare to take over the world's governments and its courts."[13] Rushdoony's lengthy work *The Institutes of Biblical Law* presents the thesis that the Law of God is operative today and must govern all society.[14]

Active Passive Obedience of Christ

Another important teaching in theonomy is the view that Christ's sufferings in His life were as substitutionary as His suffering on the cross. Theonomists along with covenant-Reformed thinkers teach that the Savior's obedience to the Law earned righteousness for His people just as Adam's obedience to God's commands to him would have earned salvation for him and his posterity. On this point, theonomy and dispensationalism are at variance.[15]

Bahnsen expressed theonomy's view of Christ's active obedience in His life this way: "Christ's perfect obedience to the Law of God secures our release from the necessity of personally keeping the law as a condition of justification."[16] Because Christ's active obedience was vicarious, the believer is therefore released from the law's condemnation through his faith, though his faith does not nullify the law. "The law brought bondage, but Christ brings redemptive freedom from sin and death (Gal. 3:23-29). Christ did this by subjecting Himself to the law. He then redeems those who are enslaved to the law and under its curse (4:4-6; cf. 3:13), making them ethically able to respond to God's will."[17] Referring to his book *Theonomy in Christian Ethics*, Bahnsen wrote, "Therefore when this treatise affirms the continuing validity of every stroke of God's Law based on scriptural authority (e. g., Matt. 5:17 and following), this teaching must be kept in proper perspective. Scripture uniformly views the Law as a standard of righteousness after which we should pattern our sanctification and Christian life, but justification is never by our obedience to the Law (after the fall of Adam and Eve)."[18]

Postmillenialism

A major attendant doctrine of theonomy is a slightly revised form of postmillennialism.[19] The two usually go together, and if the one is embraced it is consistent to hold to the other. This subject deserves more attention than will be given to it in this article. However, it is important to establish the relationship between theonomy and postmillennialism because of its antithesis to premillennial dispensationalism.

Theonomists usually acknowledge that since World War I, postmillennialism has not been a popular eschatological view. They hold that its unpopularity is totally unjustified and insist that all who adhere to Reformed Christianity must take postmillennialism seriously.

We must conclude then that current day writers have

offered no good prima facie reason for ignoring or rejecting postmillennialism as an important theological option for biblical believers. It has been unwarrantedly dismissed in the past 50 years on the basis of a newspaper exegesis, misrepresentation, two-edged criticisms, and premature or unfounded charges. Postmillennialism deserves to be taken seriously and considered in the light of Scripture; quick dismissal or ignoring of it in recent years has no good justification. [20]

What in particular sets off contemporary postmillennialism from amillennialism and premillennialism? As Bahnsen explains, "The thing that distinguishes the biblical postmillennialist then from amillennialism and premillennialism is his belief that Scripture teaches the success of the great commission in this age of the church." [21] Theonomists have an "optimistic confidence" that the nations of the world "will become disciples of Christ, and [that] the church will grow to fill the earth, and that Christianity will become the dominant principle." [22] "The gospel . . . shall convert the vast majority of the world to Christ and bring widespread obedience to His kingdom rule." [23]

Chilton expresses the same postmillennial optimism. "The garden of Eden, the Mountain of the Lord will be restored in history, before the second coming, by the power of the gospel, and the desert will rejoice and blossom as the rose (Isa. 35:1)." [24] "The entire Gentile world will be converted to faith in Jesus Christ. The mass of the Gentiles will come into the covenant until the conversion of the Gentiles reaches the point of *fullness.* " [25] "As the gospel progresses throughout the world it will win, and win, and win, until all kingdoms become the kingdoms of our Lord and of His Christ; and He will reign forever and ever." [26]

Rushdoony gave a summary of this view in these words:

Postmillennialism thus believes that man must be saved, and that his regeneration is the starting point for a mandate to exercise dominion in Christ's name over every

174

area of life and thought. Postmillennialism in its classic form does not neglect the church and it does not neglect also to work for a Christian state and school, for the sovereignty and crown rights of the King over individuals, families, institutions, arts, scientists, and all things else. More, it holds that God has provided the way for this conquest: His law. Every word that God speaks is law; it is binding on man. Grace, love, and law are only contraries in a pagan view; in God, they serve a common purpose, to further His kingdom and glory.[27]

DISPENSATIONALISM

Theonomy unlike dispensationalism is not a system of theology but a contemporary emphasis on the relationship of the law to the present age, stemming from covenant theology and associated integrally with the current expression of postmillennialism. But as systems of theology, dispensational theology and covenant theology stand in sharp contrast.[28]

Dispensation

The Greek word occasionally translated "dispensation" refers to an administration or stewardship (Luke 16:2-4; 1 Cor. 9:17; Eph. 1:10; 3:2, 9; Col. 1:25; 1 Tim. 1:4). (Cf. the related word in Luke 12:42; 16:1-3, 8; Rom. 16:23; 1 Cor. 4:1-2; Gal. 4:2; Titus 1:7; 1 Peter 4:10.) Each obviously involves and includes time, though that is not necessarily the most important feature of it.[29] The following definition is concise and entirely consistent with the scriptural usage of the term: "A dispensation is a distinguishable economy in the outworking of God's purpose."[30]

Dispensationalism

Building on the above definition of a dispensation, dis-

175

pensationalism may be defined as that system of theology which interprets the Bible literally—according to normal usage—and places primary emphasis on the major biblical covenants (Abrahamic, Palestinian, Davidic, New)—and sees the Bible as the unfolding of distinguishable economies in the outworking of God's major purpose to bring glory to Himself.

Covenant theology, on which theonomy is solidly based, represents a different system and yields different results. It is that system of theology which places primary emphasis on theological covenants—redemption, works, grace—viewing the biblical covenants as stages in the accomplishment of God's major purpose, which is redemptive.

Every major doctrine that is part of a system of theology is affected by premillennial dispensationalism. Some are affected more than others, of course. They are related because of the literal hermeneutic on which premillennialism and dispensationalism rest. When consistently applied throughout Scripture, this results in theological viewpoints that are at variance with covenant theology, whether it be the classic or theonomic postmillennial variety or the amillennial form or the non-dispensational premillenial form.[31]

Dispensational Variations

Not all who see distinctions in God's ways of dealing with His creatures at different times agree on when the church as a new and distinct entity began or even on the number of dispensations. However, the majority of those who gladly accept the designation "dispensational" hold that the church began on the day of Pentecost. This is usually the view of dispensationalism by which other varieties are measured.

Baker is rightly classified as a dispensationalist but does not share the view that the church began on the day of Pentecost. He finds four groupings within dispensationalism: "There are thus four major groups of dispensationalists, covenant theologians who recognize only two basic dispensations and who oppose dispensationalism as a principle of biblical interpretation, and the three groups who do recognize this principle but begin the new dispensation of the mystery at either Acts 2, Acts 13, or Acts 28.[32]

Those who classify themselves as dispensationalists but do not believe the present dispensation of the Church Age began on the day of Pentecost are often labeled ultradispensationalists or hyperdispensationalists. Commonly used by their opponents, these designations seem unfair, for they prejudice the case and are, of course, not appreciated by those of whom they are used. Ryrie identifies those who believe the church began in Acts 9 or Acts 13 as "moderate" ultradispensationalists and those who hold that it began with Acts 28 as "extreme" ultradispensationalists.[33]

The differences between those who say the church began in Acts 9, 13, or 28 and those who see it as having begun in Acts 2 must not be minimized. They are crucial and have far-reaching consequences. However, all four positions hold in common the distinction between God's program for Israel and His program for the church, and this, of course, separates all dispensationalists from nondispensationalists.

The Sine Qua Non of Dispensationalism

Granted, there are differences among dispensationalists over the number of dispensations and, as already stated, over the time when the church began. The question then becomes, What is the least common denominator? What must one believe to be classified legitimately as a dispensationalist? It certainly is not the number of distinguishable economies one holds to. Since some committed premillennialists reject dispensationalism, premillennialism is not determinative either. One must look elsewhere for the sine qua non of dispensationalism.

Friends and foes of dispensationalism must agree that the all-determinative conviction without which one cannot be a dispensationalist is the distinction between God's program for Israel and His program for the church. This distinction is based solidly on the literal (or as many dispensationalists prefer to call it, the normal) interpretation of Scripture. A consistently literal hermeneutic brings one to see distinctions in God's program with Israel and His program with the church, and that underscores the theological rather than the soteriological nature of God's primary purpose in the world.[34]

Theonomy and Dispensationalism Contrasted

Based on what has been stated, several crucial differences between theonomy and dispensationalism may be noted: (1) Theonomy is founded on covenant theology. Dispensationalism and covenant theology represent differing systems of theology. (2) Theonomy insists that no distinction exists between God's program with Israel and His program with the church. This distinction is the sine qua non of dispensationalism. (3) Theonomy believes that the Old Testament Law of God, in brief, the whole Mosaic economy, is still operative today. Dispensationalism believes that the Law of Moses as a rule of life was terminated at Calvary. (4) Theonomy does not believe in a future for Israel as a nation. Dispensationalism most assuredly does.

NOTES

1. Postmillennial theonomy finds current expression in the *Journal of Christian Reconstruction,* the Chalcedon Ministries, Christianity and Civlization, and the Geneva Divinity School Press of Tyler, Texas. Some significant contributors to the movement are Greg L. Bahnsen, James B. Jordan, Gary North, Rousas John Rushdoony, and Norma Shepherd.
2. Meredith G. Kline, "Comments on an Old-New Error," *Westminster Theological Journal* 41 (1978): 172–73.
3. R. Laird Harris, "Theonomy in Christian Ethics," *Covenant Seminary Review* 5 (1979): 1.
4. Greg L. Bahnsen, *Theonomy in Christian Ethics* (Phillipsburg, N.J.: Presbyterian and Reformed Publishing Co., 1984), 83.
5. Cited by Bahnsen, *Theonomy,* 84.
6. Ibid.

7. Ibid.
8. Ibid.
9. David Chilton, *Paradise Restored: An Eschatology of Dominion* (Tyler, Texas: Reconstruction Press, 1985), 12.
10. Ibid., 214 (italics his).
11. Ibid., 226.
12. R. J. Rushdoony, "Government and the Christian," *The Rutherford Institute* 1 (July/August 1984): 6.
13. Ibid., 7.
14. R. J. Rushdoony, *The Institutes of Biblical Law* (Nutley, N.J.: Craig Press, 1973).
15. See the author's "The Savior's Sufferings in Life," *Bibliotheca Sacra* 127 (January–March 1970): 26–37 for further discussion of this position.
16. Bahnsen, *Theonomy*, 128.
17. Ibid., 133.
18. Ibid., 135.
19. "One variety of postmillennialism is identifiable simply by a special optimism it entertains for the final stage of the preconsummation history of the church's evangelistic mission to the world. Differing little from amillennialism, that kind of postmillennialism might content itself with an appeal to passages like Romans 9–11, interpreted in a certain way, without bringing the kingdom prophecies of the Old Testament into the discussion at all. The brand of postmillennialism adopted by the Chalcedon writers includes something more. They do appeal to the prophecies that portray the messianic kingdom after the model of the visible Israelite theocratic kingdom and they interpret this prophetic picture as having fulfillment—visible, earthly fulfillment—during the millennium (which they understand as being coextensive with the preconsummation history of the New Testament church rather than a special period at the close of that church age, as many other postmillennialists view it). Thus Bahnsen maintains that the theocratic reality which fulfills those prophecies already exists and will come to increasing visibility in preconsummation history within the millennium, a universal theocracy (or Christocracy) will prevail on earth with all nations and kings serving and blessing Jesus Christ, the lamb on David's throne" (Kline, "Comments on an Old-New Error," 178–79).
20. Greg L. Bahnsen, "The Prima Facie Acceptability of Postmillennialism," *Journal of Christian Reconstruction* 3 (Winter 1976-77): 60.
21. Ibid., 68.
22. Ibid.
23. Ibid.

24. Chilton, *Paradise Restored,* 46.
25. Ibid., 129 (italics his).
26. Ibid., 192.
27. R. J. Rushdoony, "Postmillennialism versus Impotent Religion," *Journal of Christian Reconstruction* 3, (Winter 1976–77): 126 (italics his).
28. There is general agreement on both sides that dispensationalists extend the literal method beyond the major tenets of historic Christian faith—inspiration of the Bible, the deity of Christ, substitutionary atonement, salvation by grace through faith, the second coming of Christ, future resurrection and judgment—to other specific areas such as a distinction between (a) God's program with Israel and the church, (b) the rapture and the Second Coming, (c) the judgment seat of Christ and the great white throne judgment, and (d) the times of the resurrections of the saved and of the unsaved.
29. Some early dispensational writers, though not all of them, stressed the time aspect. See, for example, Scofield's definition in *The Scofield Reference Bible* (New York: Oxford University Press, 1945), 5.
30. Charles C. Ryrie, *Dispensationalism Today* (Chicago: Moody Press, 1965), 29.
31. For a contrast of these see John F. Walvoord, *The Millennial Kingdom* (Findlay, Ohio: Dunham Publishing Co., 1959), 59–295.
32. Charles F. Baker, *A Dispensational Theology* (Grand Rapids: Grace Bible College Publications, 1972), 6. Baker believes the church or present dispensation "began with the apostle Paul before he wrote his first epistle" (p. 6). After stating his own position he then sets forth five reasons why the church did not begin in Acts 2 and eight reasons why it did not begin at or after Acts 28 (6–7).
33. See Ryrie, *Dispensationalism Today,* 192–205 for a summary and an evaluation of ultradispensationalism.
34. Ibid., 43–47.

■ ■ ■ ■ ■ ■ ■ ■ ■

MEDICAL
ISSUES

13

A BIBLICAL APPRAISAL OF ARTIFICIAL REPRODUCTION

J. Kerby Anderson

Many husbands and wives who have no children are seriously considering new procedures of artificial reproduction. They argue that these procedures are no different from normal conception. "It's just a plumbing bypass," they reason.

If a couple goes to a pastor for counsel on the matter, how should the pastor respond? Major advances in the field of genetic research have ushered in a "brave new world" of medical technology. But with this new technology have come troubling ethical questions and dilemmas.

These dilemmas are exacerbated by the speed at which new medical technologies are being developed and deployed. What was science fiction yesterday has become science fact today. Consequently, doctors, lawyers, and pastors must try to "catch up" to the latest developments, and often technologies are implemented before the medical, legal, ethical, and theological implications of genetic technology are understood. This article attempts to survey the subject of artificial reproduction and to provide a biblical appraisal of these techniques.[1]

Background Information

The four most popular methods of artificial reproduction are artificial insemination (known as AIH or AID), surrogate parenting, embryo transfer, and in vitro fertilization (called IVF). The oldest and most often utilized method is artificial insemination. More than 20,000 children are born each year by means of artificial insemination. This method uses artificial means to impregnate a woman with the sperm of her husband (AIH-artificial insemination by the husband), or of a donor (AID-artificial insemination by a donor) in order to circumvent problems of male infertility.

Surrogate parenting uses artificial insemination to circumvent female infertility. A surrogate mother is artificially inseminated by the sperm of the donor father. When the child is born, the surrogate mother gives the child up to the donor father and social mother.

Embryo transfer is the newest technique to be developed and goes one step further. It uses artificial insemination to impregnate a "surrogate mother," but then early in the pregnancy the developing embryo is flushed out and implanted in the wife.

In vitro fertilization allows doctors to fertilize an egg and grow it outside the womb for a short period of time. Though scientists cannot yet grow a test-tube baby completely outside the womb, further advances in the development of an artificial placenta may enable them to fertilize and gestate an embryo outside a human womb.

The goal of providing children to childless couples is certainly commendable, but Christians are obligated to ask further questions. While the goal may be noble, the means by which this goal is achieved must be moral and must not violate biblical principles. Is this merely a plumbing bypass? First, a few scientific concerns that commentators have raised need to be examined.

Scientific Concerns

A major scientific issue centers on one's concern for human life. Procedures like IVF and embryo transfer are wasteful of fetal life and can sometimes result in premature births. According to the 1987 data from the American Fertility Society, the success rate for in vitro fertilization is 8 percent.[2] In other words, 92 out of every 100 embryos do not result in the birth of a baby. A 1985 Australian study showed that women undergoing this treatment were about three times more likely than other mothers to give birth prematurely.[3] However, once born, these children do not seem to manifest any genetic problems. In vitro children appear to be as healthy and mentally alert as infants conceived through normal reproduction.[4]

At the moment, these techniques are less effective than normal conception. Therefore the burden of proof must fall on the experimenters to guarantee the safety of the unborn child. A wife may feel she is ready to take the risk in order to have a child, but another life is involved in the equation — the child to be conceived. Do Christians have any ethical responsibility toward children conceived by this method? Further study and research are necessary before Christians could, in good conscience, counsel others to use these techniques.

Social Concerns

These procedures also raise significant social questions. An important question is, Will they lead to unintended consequences? Like many other forms of technology, they may be very beneficial, but once implemented they may create a climate in which moral choices may naturally lead to immoral consequences. A new practice brings with it particular views and values that shape the world view of those involved so that previously repugnant practices seem more reasonable. The same procedure that can provide children to married couples who desire children can also lead to other consequences.

Suppose a wife wants a child but she wants to specify its sex and physical characteristics. If she wants a boy, sex selection procedures enable physicians to separate X-sperm (which will produce a girl) from Y-sperm (which will produce a boy). There is no technological reason why this cannot be done; so most people say, Why not?

Also suppose she would like to have a child that has blond hair and blue eyes. This presents a bigger problem. Her husband has brown hair and brown eyes. But suppose she finds a neighbor with blond hair and blue eyes to donate his sperm. The doctors could therefore mix her eggs with the neighbor's sperm. Again, there is no technological reason why this could not be done; so they proceed.

Also assume that before the fertilized embryo is placed in the wife, she has a physical examination and finds that she should not carry another child because of a health problem. So she simply asks another neighbor to carry the child as a surrogate mother.

So here is a male neighbor's sperm mixed with the wife's egg and placed in a female neighbor's body. Three seemingly simple decisions have led to an unusual conclusion. Think of the legal questions. For example, who is the father—the neighbor or the woman's husband? Who is the mother—the woman or her neighbor? What should be done if the neighbor carrying the baby decides to keep the child after it is born? Moreover, what about the moral questions? Has adultery taken place? Has something immoral happened?

Answers to these questions are difficult because the meaning of human parenthood is now changed in such a profound way that standard societal and biblical categories are blurred. The slide from this relatively plausible scenario down the slope toward more fearful ones is quite possible.

This in fact was the central premise in the novel *Brave New World* written by Aldous Huxley in 1932. His vision for the future was a dystopia (the opposite of utopia). He feared that technology, especially genetic technology, would create a world of tyranny. He envisioned a world dominated by and controlled by genetic engineers who created future generations in their own image and forsook the traditional forms of human procreation and parenting. Certainly some of these new forms of artificial reproduction move us closer to that possibility.

Almost daily, new advances in artificial reproduction further erode the biblical categories of marriage, procreation, and family. In South Africa, a grandmother gave birth to her daughter's triplets. Four of her daughter's eggs were fertilized in the laboratory and implanted in the grandmother's womb. Three developed and she gave birth to her own grandchildren.[5]

In the United States, researchers have developed a technique in animals that will soon allow lesbian couples to have children. Already lesbians have used artificial insemination to provide children for their "marriages." A research scientist at Vanderbilt University developed a technique which, if perfected, would allow doctors to take an unfertilized egg from one woman and fuse it with an egg from another woman and produce a baby girl genetically related to both women.[6] This would provide lesbians with an ability to produce female children without any male involvement!

A married woman may simply desire to have a child. But unless there are strict controls on the application of artificial insemination, will society not slide into these very bizarre consequences? Leon Kass, of the National Academy of Sciences, sees artificial reproduction as "a giant step towards the full laboratory control of human reproduction."[7] The technology is available to fertilize eggs and implant them in any womb. Advances in storage techniques for genetic materials give the possibility of mixing sperm and egg from people in different continents or even from people who are not living.

Any technology can be used for good or evil. Christians are to exercise dominion (Gen. 1:28) and to control technology so that good rather than evil results. Christians therefore should speak out against bizarre reproductive variations, or else the scientific community will continue to perfect their application. Christians should support the treatment of infertility but must not allow society to use such advances to foster programs of artificial reproduction for deviant sexual lifestyles.

Moral Concerns

An important moral concern centers on the place of reproductive technology in today's society. If mistakes are made in human reproduction, future generations will have to bear the consequences. Does the medical world know enough to tamper with human reproduction?

A childless wife may claim that using artificial reproduction is no more controversial than heart bypass surgery, but it seems to be much more. In a heart bypass operation the goal is to cure the patient, and the surgery is done only as a last resort with proper consent of the patient. Artificial reproductive techniques are done to cater to the desires of a couple without the consent of the person who may be most affected (the child) and with the prospect of significant social consequences.

Pastors should encourage their counselees to pursue other less expensive and less ethically questionable options first. Here are five other options these couples should consider.

First, a woman may consider the possibility of tuboplasty, in which the fallopian tubes are repaired or reconstructed. Microsurgery can restore fertility in 70 percent of women with minor scarring around their tubes.[8]

Second, a couple may consider adoption. Nearly three-fourths of all couples are willing to consider adoption, and some experts estimate that as many as 500,000 children are eligible for adoption in this country.[9]

A third option is drug treatment. A number of drugs are now becoming available to aid in various fertility problems. These drugs can regulate a woman's menstrual cycle and vastly improve her chances of becoming pregnant.

A fourth option (still experimental) is a procedure known as low tubal ovum transfer. A laparoscope is used to remove an egg from the ovary and then implant it by means of a syringe into a fallopian tube on the other side of the blockage. Since the subsequent fertilization is done in vivo, many of the concerns raised in this paper are no longer a consideration.

A final option is to remain childless. Children are a "gift of the Lord" (Ps. 127:3), but that does not mean it is wrong to be single or to be married and childless. Because of the Fall (Gen. 3), medical abnormalities such as infertility exist. God has called men to exercise dominion over creation, but that does not sanction the use of all forms of technology. If a medical defect can be corrected with an ethically acceptable medical technology, then such procedures should be utilized. If one is not available, then being childless should not be a disgrace. Couples should recognize that God is sovereign over procreation. In the Old Testament, Hannah sought the Lord for a child (1 Sam. 1).

Theological Concerns

A major theological concern with certain artificial reproductive procedures is their threat to the basis for the sanctity of human life. Man is created in God's image (Gen. 1:27), and God's special care and protection extend even to unborn children (Ps. 139).

In vitro fertilization and embryo transfer violate this sanctity in three ways. First, there is the potential loss of fetal life. Even with the newer and more successful techniques, there is still a considerable loss of fertilized ova. Second, there is a general practice of destroying fertilized ova if they appear abnormal. Third, there has been the practice of hyperfertilization. Many eggs are fertilized simultaneously, one is selected for implantation, and the others are thrown away. Until protection of the unborn child can be guaranteed, Christians must question these practices.

A second theological issue is the effect various forms of artificial reproduction have on a biblical view of sexual relations within marriage. These procedures separate the physical dimensions of sexual intercourse from the emotional and spiritual ones.

A procedure like artificial insemination by the husband (AIH) does not seem to raise significant theological concerns, since the pregnancy results from the sperm of the husband. In a procedure like artificial insemination of a donor (AID), the intervention of a third party into the pregnancy has occured but is less visible, since both marriage partners must consent to

189

the procedure and conception is achieved through insemination from an anonymous sperm donor. Yet many Christians have moral concerns even with this procedure.

But the intervention of a third party in the marriage becomes more pronounced when surrogate parenting and embryo transfer are involved. These procedures dehumanize prenatal care for infants and open up a realm of commercialization of parenting (leading inevitably to "wombs for rent"). In the end these new reproductive alternatives hold the prospect of "turning the marriage bed into a chemistry set."

A third theological issue is the biblical view of parenthood. Human parenthood involves two spheres: the unitive (Gen. 2:24) and the procreative (1:28). These are tied together by the union of sexuality, love, and procreation. "Making love" and "making babies" (to use vernacular terms) are tied to the same physical act. The pleasure of sex, the communication of love, and the desire for children are unified in the same act. Artificial reproduction frequently separates these functions and thus poses a potential threat to the completeness God intended for marriage.

Motherhood may also be affected. Childbearing would no longer be a natural outcome of procreation. The proliferation of surrogate mothers will continue to blur the true relationship between procreation and parenthood. God intends that the family thrive (Eph. 6:1-4; Col. 3:18-21), and these genetic advances pose a threat to the stability of the family.

By contrast, a family can survive without children. God determines birth (Gen. 4:1; 17:16; Ruth 4:13) and is in control even over barren wombs (Deut. 7:14). Childless women are not displeasing to God, as the testimonies of Sarah (Gen. 18), Rachel (Gen. 29–30), and Hannah (1 Sam. 1) attest. God is in control and can bring great blessing out of the heartbreak of infertility.

Though artificial reproduction offers hope for infertile couples, more careful attention must be given to these scientific, social, moral, and theological issues. Unless further research can assure medical safety and unless social controls are implemented that will prevent the social ills raised here, Christians would be wise to withold their support of many of these genetic procedures.

NOTES

1. A more detailed discussion of this area can be found in the author's book *Genetic Engineering* (Grand Rapids: Zondervan Publishing House, 1982).

2. "In vitro: A look at process," *USA Today*, 11 August 1989, 3A.

3. "45% of Test-Tube Pregnancies in Study Failed," *Dallas Morning News*, 27 October 1985, 29A.

4. "Test-tube children normal, study finds," *Dallas Morning News*, 10 August 1989.

5. "Mother Bears Triplets for Her Daughter," *San Francisco Chronicle*, 8 April 1987, 24.

6. Lori Andrews, "Embryo Technology," *Parents*, May 1981, 69.

7. Leon Kass, "Making Babies Revisited," *Public Interest* 54 (Winter 1979): 29–54.

8. Claudia Wallis, "The New Origins of Life," *Time*, 10 September 1984, 48.

9. Richard Cohen, "Test Tube Babies: Why Add to a Surplus?" *Washington Post*, 3 February 1980, B-1.

14

A BIBLICAL APPRAISAL OF EUTHANASIA

J. Kerby Anderson

P astors and physicians alike agonize over the ethics of euthanasia. Is it moral to withhold medical treatment from a terminally ill patient? Is it ever right to "pull the plug" on a patient? These are only two of the many ethical questions surrounding the practice of euthanasia.

The term *euthanasia* was coined (in its currently prominent sense) by historian W.E.H. Lecky in 1869. Derived from the Greek words for "happy death" or "good death," the term *euthanasia* traditionally conveyed the idea of keeping terminally ill patients free from pain in their last days. Unfortunately, in recent years it has come to mean a great deal many other things.

This change in definition is well illustrated by the standard dictionary definition of euthanasia used in most courts. Webster's Dictionary provides two definitions: (1) "an easy death or means of inducing one" and (2) "the act or practice of painlessly putting to death persons suffering from incurable conditions or diseases."[1]

This definition immediately reflects the problem with a discussion of euthanasia. Euthanasia means different things to different people. Most lay people once assumed the focus was merely on what can properly be called "palliative care," which includes attempts by doctors and nurses to ease pain in terminal patients, but does not mean "inducing death." But to many people today, euthanasia includes not just a passive management of pain but an active termination of a suffering patient's life by a second party.

Thus, crucial to any discussion of euthanasia is a proper understanding of the various forms of euthanasia. Under this broader definition of euthanasia are some practices that can be justified from a biblical perspective while many others are clearly immoral and even criminal in nature.

FORMS OF EUTHANASIA

Ethical and medical discussions of euthanasia frequently include various forms of treatment or lack of treatment that fall under the general term *euthanasia*. Four categories of euthanasia are frequently discussed in medical literature.

1. Voluntary, passive euthanasia. This form of euthanasia assumes that medical personnel, at the patient's request, will merely allow nature to take its course. In the past, passive euthanasia meant that the physician did nothing to hasten death but did provide care, comfort, and counsel to dying patients.[2]

2. Voluntary, active euthanasia. This means that the physician, by request, hastens death by taking some active means (e.g., lethal injection). There is also the controversial issue of whether nonmedical personnel such as a spouse or friend can be permitted to end the suffering of another.[3]

3. Involuntary, passive euthanasia. This assumes that the patient has not expressed a willingness to die or cannot do so. The medical personnel do not go to any extraordinary measures to save the patient but they often withhold food (by removing nasogastric tubes), antibiotics, or life-support systems (respirator).

4. Involuntary, active euthanasia. This begins to blur into homocide. The physician does something active to hasten death, regardless of the patient's wishes, for "humanitarian" reasons, economic considerations, or genetic justifications.

ANALYSIS OF DIFFERENT FORMS OF EUTHANASIA

An analysis of the moral questions in each form of euthanasia needs to be made. Each form has its own unique set of issues.

Voluntary, Passive Euthanasia

This is not truly euthanasia in the modern sense. In these situations it is assumed that death is imminent and inevitable. At this point the medical personnel's attention turns from curing the disease to making the patient as comfortable as possible. Further medical treatment to prolong life becomes pointless and an entirely different medical strategy is implemented.

This medical strategy is frequently referred to as palliative care. The prime focus is on alleviating pain, while not actually curing the patient.

Medications that deaden pain but do not dim consciousness can be administered. Medical personnel can give the patient the so-called Brompton's cocktail, which consists of morphine, cocaine, alcohol, syrup, and chloroform water in order to deaden pain but allow conscious activity.

Certain patients can even be released to hospices where they can spend their last days with family and friends rather than in a clinical hospital setting. The hospice program provides a coordinated program of doctors, nurses, and special consultants who help the dying patient and his family through their time of struggle.

But even this form of euthanasia is not without its controversy. Many physicians are reluctant to discontinue medical efforts to cure terminal patients. Their reluctance is not so much driven by a belief that they will be successful as it is by their concern about possible malpractice suits from the family. Patients who are ready "to go to be with the Lord" may find themselves at odds with doctors who are fearful they may have to prove in a court of law that they did "all they could" for the patient.

Stepping into this legal/ethical dilemma has been the Presi-

194

dent's Commission for the Study of Ethical Problems in Medicine. The Commission came to the following conclusions concerning terminally ill patients.[4] (1) The Commission stated that a terminally ill patient generally should have the right to choose to die without interference from lawyers, legislators, or bureaucrats. (2) The Commission believes that patients suffering loss of consciousness should have the type of care that is dictated largely by their families' wishes. (3) Resuscitation need not always be attempted on a hospitalized patient whose heart stops. Patients likely to suffer cardiac arrest should be informed before the operation and allowed to decide in advance for or against resuscitation. (4) Patients should have greater rights to give instructions in advance of becoming incapacitated. They should have the right to appoint a proxy to carry out their wishes.

These conclusions of the President's Commission have provided the basis for revision of state laws governing medical care of the terminally ill. In general they provide doctors with greater latitude in making decisions concerning dying patients. But they do raise significant questions for Christians.

First, is there such a thing as a "right to die"? From a Christian perspective, this is certainly questionable (as discussed later in this article under "Biblical Analysis"). But it also raises important legal questions never addressed by the founders of this country nor by modern courts. While the Declaration of Independence does recognize a "right to life," it does not recognize (nor even assume) a "right to die."

Second, the conclusions suggest that a patient's decisions about life and death can be done by proxy. In most cases this has been done through a legal instrument known as "the living will" or through a "durable power of attorney" (DPOA). Presently 35 states allow individuals to draw up a legal document known as a "living will," in which they specify their desires regarding medical treatment if they become terminally ill and incompetent. A DPOA gives a third party, or proxy, power to make decisions on behalf of the patient. In the past these covered only financial decisions, but court precedents have extended these to cover health-care decisions as well.

The fundamental problem with these proxy arrangements is that they are usually based on some "quality of life" standard. Yet a Christian perspective on human life sees all life as sacred and given by God. Decisions about life and death should be governed by a "sanctity of life" standard rather than by a "quality of life" standard.

Voluntary, Active Euthanasia

This implies that something is done to hasten death. This raises both moral and legal questions. Does active euthanasia constitute an act of murder or assisted suicide? Or is it merely a compassionate act of "mercy killing"?

It is helpful to distinguish between mercy killing and what could be called mercy dying. Taking a human life is not the same as allowing nature to take its course by allowing a terminal patient to die. The former is immoral (and perhaps even criminal), while the latter is not.

However, drawing a sharp line between these two categories is not as easy as it used to be. Modern medical technology has significantly blurred the line between hastening death and allowing nature to take its course. Certain analgesics, for example, not only ease pain, but can also shorten a patient's life (by affecting respiration). An artificial heart will continue to beat even after the patient has died and therefore must be turned off by the doctor. So the distinction between actively promoting death and passively allowing nature to take its course is sometimes difficult to determine in practice. But this fundamental distinction between life-taking and death-permitting is still an important philosophical distinction.

Another concern with active euthanasia is that it eliminates the possibility for recovery. While this should be obvious, somehow this problem is frequently ignored in the euthanasia debate. Terminating a human life eliminates all possibility of recovery, while passively ceasing extraordinary means may not. Miraculous recovery from a bleak prognosis sometimes occurs. A doctor who prescribes active euthanasia for a patient may unwittingly prevent a possible recovery he did not anticipate.

A further concern with this so-called voluntary, active euthanasia is that these decisions might not always be freely made. The possibility for coercion is always present. A few years ago, Richard D. Lamm, former governor of Colorado, said that elderly, terminally ill patients have "a duty to die and get out of the way." Though those words were reported somewhat out of context, they nonetheless illustrate the pressure many elderly feel from hospital personnel.

Former Surgeon General C. Everett Koop has said that proponents of active euthanasia "have gotten across to a whole segment of the elderly population that somehow because they are living, they are depriving someone else of a prior right to resources. That is a most reprehensible thing." He added, "When I was doing research for *Whatever Happened to the Human Race?* I went to nursing homes and talked to people who felt that pressure. Old people were apologizing to me for using a bed, for being alive, for taking medication, because they knew somebody else deserved it more. I think that's pitiful."[5]

Involuntary, Passive Euthanasia

This form of euthanasia is an act of omission in which medical personnel do not go to any extraordinary measures to save the patient. This can be a morally acceptable omission when dealing with terminal patients.

Unfortunately, this omission often includes actions that are more accurately described as active euthanasia. Withholding food (by removing nasogastric tubes), antibiotics, or life-support procedures (respirator) is much more than passive euthanasia. As already mentioned, candidates for euthanasia have been known to make miraculous recoveries, but such a possibility is eliminated when a patient is starved to death.

Sometimes, however, decisions must be made about "pulling the plug." A comatose patient without any brain wave activity (a flat EEG, electroencephalogram) should be removed from life-support systems; he is considered to be already dead. But in other situations a comatose patient might recover. These difficult decisions should be left up to the neurophysiologist who can evaluate a patient's prognosis. But in general, one may assume that the patient will recover and therefore life-support systems should be continued, thus placing the burden of proof on those who wish to "pull the plug."

Motives behind involuntary euthanasia are frequently mixed. Are the medical personnel recommending euthanasia because of bed shortages or depleted medical facilities? Or are they suggesting euthanasia out of a compassionate concern for the patient? Is a son, for example, agreeing to euthanasia out of concern for his mother's well-being or out of a desire to gain her inheritance?

The mixed motives behind these decisions are not easy to sort out, and they add further moral and legal questions to the medical landscape. Motives are clearer when nature is allowed to take its course, and agonizing decisions are not thrust on the patient or family about "when to pull the plug."

Involuntary, Active Euthanasia

In this form, a second party makes decisions about whether active measures should be taken to end a life. Foundational to this discussion is an erosion of the doctrine of the sanctity of life. But ever since the Supreme Court ruled in *Roe vs. Wade* that the lives of unborn babies could be terminated for reasons of convenience, society's slide down this slippery moral slope has continued.

The progression was inevitable. Once society begins to devalue the life of an unborn child, it is but a small step to begin to do the same with a child that has been born. Abortion slides naturally into infanticide and eventually into euthanasia. In the past few years doctors have allowed a number of so-called "Baby Does" to die (either by failing to perform lifesaving operations or else by failing to feed the infants). And governmental attempts to prevent such practices have been overruled by the courts.[6]

Further progression toward euthanasia is inevitable. Once society becomes conformed to a "quality of life" standard for infants, it will more willingly accept the same standard for the elderly. As C. Everett Koop has said, "Nothing surprises me anymore. My great concern is that there will be 10,000 Grandma Does for every Baby Doe."[7]

Once human life is devalued, all sorts of actions defined as "euthanasia" can be justified. This is precisely what happened in Nazi Germany and can happen in this country as well. Ethicist Yale Kamisar provides this descriptive progression of events:

> Miss Voluntary Euthanasia is not likely to be going it alone for very long. Many of her admirers . . . would be neither surprised nor distressed to see her joined by Miss Euthanize the Congenital Idiots and Miss Euthanize the Permanently Insane and Miss Euthanize the Senile Dementia. And these lasses, whether or not they themselves constitute a "parade of horrors," certainly make excellent majorettes for such a parade.[8]

BIBLICAL ANALYSIS

Foundational to a biblical perspective on euthanasia is a proper understanding of the sanctity of human life. For centuries Western culture in general and Christians in particular have believed in the sanctity of human life. Unfortunately, this view is beginning to erode into a "quality of life" standard. Before, the disabled, retarded, and infirm were seen as having a special place in God's world; but today medical personnel judge a person's fitness for life on the basis of a perceived quality of life or lack of such quality.

No longer is life seen as sacred and worthy of being saved.

Now patients are evaluated and lifesaving treatment frequently denied based on a subjective and arbitrary standard for the supposed quality of life. If a life is not judged worthy to be lived any longer, people feel obliged to end that life.

Western society must return to the fundamental belief that because man is created in the image of God (Gen. 1:27; 5:1-2), all human life is sacred. Society must not place an arbitrary standard of quality above God's absolute standard of human value and worth. This does not mean that people will no longer need to make difficult decisions about treatment and care, but it does mean that these decisions will be guided by an objective, absolute standard of human worth.

Another foundational principle involves a biblical view of life-taking. The Bible specifically condemns murder (Ex. 20:13), and this would surely include active forms of euthanasia in which another person (doctor, nurse, or friend) hastens death in a patient. While there are situations described in Scripture in which life-taking may be permitted (e.g., self-defense or a just war), euthanasia should not be included with any of these established biblical categories. Active euthanasia, like murder, involves premeditated intent and therefore should be condemned as immoral and even criminal.

Christians should also reject the attempt by the modern euthanasia movement to promote a so-called "right to die." Secular society's attempt to establish this "right to die" is wrong for two reasons. First, giving a person a right to die is tantamount to promoting suicide, and suicide is condemned in the Bible. Man is forbidden to murder and that includes murder of oneself. Moreover, Christians are commanded to love others as they love themselves (Matt. 22:39; Eph. 5:29). Implicit in the command is an assumption of self-love as well as love for others.

Suicide, however, is hardly an example of self-love; it is usually a selfish act. People kill themselves to get away from pain and problems, often leaving those problems to friends and family members who must pick up the pieces when the one who committed suicide is gone.

Second, this so-called "right to die" denies God the opportunity to work sovereignly within a shattered life and bring glory to Himself. When Joni Eareckson Tada realized that she would be spending the rest of her life as a quadriplegic, she asked in despair, "Why can't they just let me die?" When her friend Diana, trying to provide comfort, said to her, "The past is dead, Joni; you're alive," Joni responded, "Am I? This isn't living."[9]

But through God's grace Joni's despair gave way to her firm conviction that even her accident was within God's plan for her life. Now she shares with the world her firm conviction that "suffering gets us ready for heaven."[10]

Another foundational principle is a biblical view of death. Modern medicine defines death primarily as a biological event; yet Scripture defines death as a spiritual event that has biological consequences. Death, according to the Bible, occurs when the spirit leaves the body (Ecc. 12:7; James 2:26).

Unfortunately, this does not offer much by way of clinical diagnosis for medical personnel. But it does suggest that a rigorous medical definition for death be used. A comatose patient may not be conscious, but from both a medical and biblical perspective he is very much alive and treatment should be continued unless brain activity has ceased.

On the other hand, Christians must also reject the notion that everything must be done to save life at all costs. Believers, knowing that to be at home in the body is to be away from the Lord (2 Cor. 5:6), long for the time when they will be absent from the body and at home with the Lord (2 Cor. 5:8). Death is gain for Christians (Phil. 1:21). Therefore they need not be so tied to this earth that they perform futile operations just to extend life a few more hours or days.

In a patient's last days, everything possible should be done to alleviate physical and emotional pain. Giving drugs to a patient to relieve pain is morally justifiable. Proverbs 31:6 says, "Give strong drink to him who is perishing, and wine to him whose life is bitter" (NASB). As previously mentioned, some analgesics have the secondary effect of shortening life.

But these should be permitted since the primary purpose is to relieve pain, even though they may secondarily shorten life.

Moreover, believers should provide counsel and spiritual care to dying patients (Gal. 6:2). Frequently, emotional needs can be met both in the patient and in the family. Such times of grief also provide opportunities for witnessing. Those suffering loss are often more open to the Gospel than at any other time.

Difficult philosophical and biblical questions are certain to continue swirling around the issue of euthanasia. But in the midst of these confusing issues should be the objective, absolute standards of Scripture, which provide guidance for the hard choices of providing care to terminally ill patients.

NOTES

1. *Webster's Third New International Dictionary of the English Language* (Springfield, Mass.: G. & C. Merriam & Co., 1971), s.v. "Euthanasia," 786.

2. A further discussion of the care and counseling of dying patients can be found in the author's book *Life, Death, and Beyond* (Grand Rapids: Zondervan Publishing House, 1980).

3. Perhaps the most famous case illustrating this form of euthanasia involved Roswell Gilbert, a 76-year-old retired electronics engineer living in Fort Lauderdale, Florida. His wife Emily had Alzheimer's disease and advancing osteoporosis. He shot her two times in what he said was a mercy killing. But he was sentenced to 25 years in prison with no chance of parole.

4. "Commission Upholds Right to Choose to Die," *Moody Monthly,* June 1983, 108.

5. Interview with Surgeon General C. Everett Koop in a "Focus on the Family" radio broadcast, aired in 1986.

6. President Reagan ordered the Department of Health and Human Services to act under Section 504 of the 1973 Rehabilitation Act to protect the lives of handicapped infants. The regulations issued by then Secretary Richard Schwieker were overturned in a U.S. District Court in 1983 and upheld by the U.S. Supreme Court in 1986.

7. Interview with Koop, "Focus on the Family" radio broadcast.

8. Yale Kamisar, "Some Non-Religious Views against Proposed Mercy Killing Legislation," *Minnesota Law Review* 22 (May 1958): 1031.

A BIBLICAL APPRAISAL OF EUTHANASIA

9. Joni Eareckson, *Joni* (Grand Rapids: Zondervan Publishing House, 1976).

10. Joni Eareckson, *A Step Further* (Grand Rapids: Zondervan Publishing House, 1978).

15

A BIBLICAL APPRAISAL OF THE ABORTION EPIDEMIC

J. Carl Laney

A bortions last year terminated one-third of all pregnancies in America. Since the Supreme Court's decision of 1973 *(Roe vs. Wade),* the annual number of abortions performed in the United States has risen from 744,600 to 1.6 million.[1] Since 1973 an estimated 21 million unborn babies have died in hospitals and abortion clinics throughout America. Nontherapeutic abortion is, in fact, a 20th-century form of birth control. It has become the second most common surgical procedure, circumcision being the first.

Abortion on demand is without question the greatest moral issue facing America today. No other contemporary moral problem in this country results in the deaths of over a million innocent, unborn children each year.

Many Christians today are not sufficiently informed about abortion to form a scripturally based opinion on this issue. Others would like to remain neutral. They do not advocate abortion, but would not prohibit a woman from having one. In an interview on abortion, a California physician stated, "I feel I have the obligation to take care of patients. I don't feel I should enforce my own personal views, especially since I'm not so convinced that [abortion] is ungodly or unbiblical."[2] Still others would identify with the "pro-choice" crusaders who contend that abortion is a right that women must have. They would argue that all other rights—social, economic, political—

depend on the fundamental right of a woman to control her own body.[3]

Abortion is a contemporary moral problem that must be addressed scripturally. The purpose of this article is to provide sufficient biblical truth and factual data to enable the reader to formulate not only a scriptural view on the abortion issue, but also a plan of action to help end the silent holocaust.

WHAT IS AN ABORTION?

Abortion is the act of bringing forth young prematurely.[4] A spontaneous abortion is one which takes place naturally — a situation over which the mother has no control. This is often referred to as a miscarriage. An induced abortion, however, is one which is brought about by medical means. In the hospitals and abortion clinics in America the term is used to refer to the destruction of the unborn child in the womb or the extraction of the immature child from the womb in order to end its life. Induced abortion is a violent act that not only destroys the life of the child but also endangers the life of the mother.[5] The methods of abortion include the following:

Suction Aspiration

Suction aspiration is a procedure used in 80 percent of the abortions up to the 12th week of pregnancy. The mouth of the cervix is dilated. A hollow tube with a knifelike edged tip is inserted into the womb. A suction force 28 times stronger than a vacuum cleaner literally tears the developing baby to pieces and sucks the remains into a container.

Dilation and Curettage

Dilation and curettage (commonly called D & C) is a procedure that involves dilating the cervix with a series of instruments to allow the insertion of a curette—a loop-shaped knife—into the womb. The instrument is used to scrape the placenta from the uterus and then cut the baby apart. The pieces are then drawn through the cervix. The tiny body must then be reassembled by an attending nurse to make sure no parts remain in the womb to cause infection.

Saline Injection

Saline injection, also known as "salt-poisoning," is an abortion procedure that involves removing some of the amniotic fluid surrounding the baby and replacing it with a toxic, saline solution. The baby then breathes and swallows the solution. In one or two hours the unborn child dies from salt poisoning, dehydration, and hemorrhaging. The mother goes into labor about 24 hours later and delivers a dead (or dying) baby.

Hysterotomy

During the last three months of pregnancy, abortions are performed by hysterotomy, which involves opening the womb surgically and removing the baby as in a cesarean section. However, the purpose of this procedure is to end the infant's life. Instead of being cared for, the baby is wrapped in a blanket, set aside, and allowed to die.

Prostaglandin

This abortion procedure involves the use of chemicals developed by the Upjohn Pharmaceutical Company. Prostaglandin hormones, injected into the womb or released in a vaginal suppository, cause the uterus to contract and deliver the child prematurely—too young to survive. A saline solution is sometimes injected first, killing the baby before birth, to make the procedure less distressful for the mother and medical staff.

The abortion procedures described above are not pleasant. But Christians need to know that when someone exercises "freedom of choice" with regard to abortion, these are the choices involved. It is remarkable that the law protects animals from cruel deaths. A person can kill his dog or cat, but he cannot kill it with cruelty. He would be subject to arrest if he cut off his pet's limbs, dissolved its skin in acid, or starved it to death. Yet the law allows these kinds of atrocities to be carried out against the most defenseless members of the human family.

Do the unborn feel pain during these abortion procedures? Yes, they do. Dr. A.W. Liley, world-renowned professor of fetal physiology at the National Women's Hospital in Auckland, New Zealand, has shown that the unborn child can feel pain and is sensitive to touch, light, heat, and noise as early as 11 weeks after conception.[6] Using closed-circuit television cameras, he has shown that if an unborn child is pricked with a needle, the infant will recoil in pain. But if a beep sounds before the prick, and this is repeated several times, the tiny baby will begin to recoil at the beep in anticipation of the pain he knows will come.

In addition to ending the life of the child, abortion endangers the life of the mother. The popular opinion that abortion is safer than childbirth is absolutely false. Published reports of deaths resulting from legal abortions range from 1.2 to 75 deaths per 100,000 abortions.[7] In the late stages of pregnancy, abortion is far more dangerous than childbirth. Death can result from uterine infection, peritonitis, hemorrhage, perforated uterus, or later tubal pregnancy.[8] Other complications relate to damage done to the cervix, injury to the lining of the womb, and blockage of the fallopian tubes. These include prematurity in subsequent pregnancies, increased miscarriages, and sterility.[9]

WHAT HAS BEEN THE LEGAL SITUATION?

On January 22, 1973, the United States Supreme Court made a seven-to-two decision on the *Roe vs. Wade* case which virtually established abortion as a constitutional right. The Court granted an absolute right to abortion on demand during the first two trimesters of pregnancy, and an almost unqualified right to abortion for "health reasons" during the third trimester. Such "health reasons," as defined in the *Doe vs. Bolton* case, include the psychological, social, and economic well-being of the mother. Harold O.J. Brown, chairman of the Christian Action Council, has pointed out:

> This places the United States alone among all the civilized nations of the world in permitting abortions at such a late point in pregnancy that the fetus, if born prematurely or by normal cesarean section at that time, would live. Such late abortions are considered in most nations of the world to be infanticide.[10]

Amazingly, in dealing with the *Roe vs. Wade* case, the Court was unwilling to decide whether or not an unborn child is fully human, yet they were willing to open the abortion floodgates.[11] Twenty-one million babies have been aborted since 1973.

On July 3, 1989 the U.S. Supreme Court upheld in a 5-4 decision a Missouri law restricting abortions. The preamble of the Missouri Act declares that "the life of each human being begins at conception."

The Missouri law (1) bars public employees from assisting in abortions and prohibits abortions from being performed in state hospitals or other publicly owned or leased facilities, (2) prohibits the use of public funds to encourage or counsel a woman to have an abortion not necessary to save her life, and (3) requires that physicians conduct viability tests before performing abortions of 20 or more weeks gestational age.

At least 22 states are likely to adopt similar prolife legislation. Abortion laws in 12 states will probably remain unchanged while 16 will become fierce battlegrounds.

WHAT DOES THE WORD OF GOD SAY?

What does the Bible have to say about abortion? Does Scripture attribute equal value to the life of an adult and the life of an unborn child? From God's perspective, is an unborn baby a human being? These are questions every Christian must wrestle with in formulating an opinion on the issue of abortion.

The Absence of a Prohibition Against Abortion

Since Scriptures have no command, "Thou shalt not have an abortion," some Christians have concluded that an induced abortion is not morally wrong or unbiblical. In response to such thinking, Cline states, "The most significant thing about abortion legislation in biblical law is that there is none. It was so unthinkable that an Israelite woman should desire an abortion that there was no need to mention this offense in the criminal code."[12] Why was abortion an unthinkable act for the ancient Israelites? First, children were recognized as a gift or heritage from the Lord (Gen. 33:5; Ps. 113:9; 127:3). Second, God was considered the One who opens the womb and allows conception (Gen. 29:33; 30:22; 1 Sam. 1:19-20). Third, childlessness was thought to be a curse, for the husband's family name could not be carried on (Deut. 25:6; Ruth 4:5). Barrenness meant the extinction of the family name (cf. Jer. 11:10). Induced abortion was so abhorrent to the Israelite mind that it was not necessary to have a specific prohibition to deal with it in the Law. Sufficient was the command, "You shall not murder" (Ex. 20:13).

Interestingly, ancient Assyrian laws attest to the abhorrence of abortion even by heathen nations near Israel. According to those laws, a woman guilty of an abortion was condemned to be impaled on stakes. Even if she lost her life in the abortion procedure, she was still to be impaled as an expression of the community's repudiation of such an abominable practice.[13] What a commentary on the moral decay of the United States that while pagan Assyrians condemned abortion, enlightened

209

"Christian" America has condoned it.

The Misinterpretation of Exodus 21:22-25

Some Christians have concluded from Exodus 21:22-25 that the fetus is merely potential human life. They understand the passage to refer to a case of accidental miscarriage. According to this view, a mere fine is levied in the case of an accidental miscarriage, whereas the law of retaliation is applied if the mother is injured or dies. It is concluded that since the punishment for accidentally killing an unborn child is less severe than the punishment for killing an adult, the unborn baby must be considered less than human,[14] Abortion, therefore, according to these persons, does not constitute the termination of "human" life and is not to be viewed as unscriptural.

This approach has two major difficulties—one in the interpretation of the text and the other in the application of the text. The usual Hebrew word for "miscarry" (Gen. 31:38; Ex. 23:26; Job 3:16; Hosea 9:14) is not used in Exodus 21:22. The verb which the New American Standard Bible translates "she has a miscarriage" (literally, "her children come out") customarily refers in the Old Testament to live births (cf. Gen. 25:26; 38:28-30; Job 3:11; 10:18; Jer. 1:5; 20:18).

On the basis of careful exegesis, Jackson concludes that "Exodus 21:22 must refer to live birth."[15] The late German commentators Keil and Delitzsch agree that it is better to take Exodus 21:22 as referring not to accidental miscarriage but to premature birth.[16]

It must also be noted that the text itself makes no distinction between harm done to the child and harm done to the mother.[17] In verse 22 two possible situations are contemplated—an accident in which no harm comes to the mother or child and an accident in which the mother or child is injured. The accident without injury results in a mere fine, probably imposed because of the danger to which the mother and child are exposed. In the case of an accident with some injury—to the mother, her child, or both—the law of retaliation is to be applied. The renowned Jewish scholar, Umberto Cassuto, translates the text as meaning premature birth: "But if any mischief happen, that is, if the woman dies or the children die, then you shall give life for life, eye for eye."[18] Frame provides a helpful paraphrase of the text under consideration:

> And if men fight together and hurt a pregnant woman so that her child is born prematurely, yet neither mother or child is harmed, he shall surely be fined, according as the woman's husband shall lay upon him; and he shall pay as the judges determine. But if either mother or child is harmed, then thou shalt give life for life, eye for eye, tooth for tooth, hand for hand, foot for foot, burning for burning, wound for wound, stripe for stripe.[19]

A second difficulty with the "miscarriage" approach to Exodus 21:22-25 is the application of the passage to the abortion issue. Even if it could be successfully demonstrated that the text refers to accidental miscarriage rather than premature birth, it still could not be used to justify abortion. First, the injury is accidental, not intentional as in abortion. Second, though unintentional, the action was considered wrongdoing and punishable by law. Third, while the text may not expressly prohibit abortion, neither does it grant authority to perform abortion.[20]

The Divine Involvement in the Formation of the Unborn

God is active in the event of conception itself (cf. Gen. 29:31-35; 30:17-24; Ruth 4:13; 1 Sam. 1:19-20), and He is also personally involved in the formation and development of the human baby in the mother's womb. God told Jeremiah, "Before I formed you in the womb I knew you, before you were born I set you apart" (Jer. 1:5). The word *formed* is used of God's special creation of Adam (Gen. 2:7-8). When used in its secular sense, it occurs most frequently in the participial form meaning "potter"—one who forms and fashions a piece of clay into a useful vessel.[21] God fashioned Jeremiah in the womb and also set him apart for his prophetic ministry before his birth. God was actively involved in the life of Jeremiah in his prenatal state.

In the third movement of Psalm 139, David joyfully acknowledged that the Lord intricately wove him together in his mother's womb. Here David wrote of God's relationship with him while he was growing and developing before birth. The significance of this psalm is highlighted by Allen:

> The Bible never speaks of fetal life as mere chemical activity, cellular growth, or vague force. Rather, the fetus in the mother's womb is described by the psalmist in vivid pictorial language as being shaped, fashioned, molded, and woven together by the personal activity of God. That is, as God formed Adam from the dust of the ground, so He is actively involved in fashioning the fetus in the womb.[22]

Verse 13 reveals that God, the Master Craftsman, fashioned David into a living person while he was still in his mother's womb. "Yes! You created my inmost self, you knitted me together in my mother's womb" (Ps. 139:13, Roland Allen).[23] The unborn child is not just a piece of tissue, but is a human being with potential for human experience.

In verse 14 David reflects on the fact that he is the product of God's creative actions: "I give public acknowledgment to you that I am awesomely wonderful; full of wonder are Your works, and my soul knows it very well" (Allen). David reflects on the fact that while he was in the womb hidden from the eyes of men, he was never hidden from God: "My bones were never hidden from you when I was being made in secret, and skillfully wrought (as) in the depths of the earth" (v. 15, Allen). The term "skillfully wrought" is used in the participial form in Exodus 26:36 of the one who wove or embroidered the beautifully colored fabric used to screen the doorway of the tabernacle. As this special fabric was intricately and skill-fully woven, so David was exquisitely fashioned[24] by God "in the depths of the earth"—a metaphorical reference to his mother's womb.

David then refers to God's watchcare over his "unformed substance" (NASB), that is, his "embryo."[25] Allen translates, "My embryo—your eyes saw! And in your Book all (my unformed parts) were written; daily they were being fashioned when as yet the whole was not (complete)" (Ps. 139:16). The word *embryo* is a key term in the abortion controversy. In man it refers to the "prefetal product of conception up to the beginning of the third month of pregnancy."[26] David acknowledged that his embryo—from the moment of conception—was under the personal watchcare of God. Concerning the significance of Psalm 139, Ryrie comments, "Even if life in the womb is not the same as it is after birth, it is human life in a certain form. And it is life which God is intimately concerned about."[27] Psalm 139:13-16 is a strong biblical polemic against abortion, for it clearly demonstrates God's personal involvement in the creation, formation, and development of the human baby.[28]

The Humanness of the Unborn According to Scripture

According to the Bible, what uniquely distinguishes man from animals is man's creation in the image and likeness of God (Gen. 1:26-27; 5:1; 9:6). Bearing the image of God is the essence of humanness. And though God's image in man was marred at the Fall, it was not erased (cf. 1 Cor. 11:7; James 3:9). If the Bible reveals that the unborn baby is made in the image of God, then it must be concluded that the unborn child is fully human in God's sight.[29] The Protestant Reformers regarded the "image of God" in man as referring to man's immaterial nature as fashioned for rational, moral, and spiritual fellowship with God.[30] Does Scripture reveal that the unborn child possesses these characteristics?

David traces the origin of his sin with Bathsheba to his own conception: "Surely I have been a sinner from birth, sinful from the time my mother conceived me" (Ps. 51:5). The "iniquity" (KJV) and "sin"(KJV) referred to here are usually viewed as David's.[31] David is relating his sinfulness to the very inception of his life—before birth. This indicates that the moral law of God was already present and operative in David in his prenatal state. Since Scripture attributes moral guilt to David as an unborn child, a strong likelihood exists that he was human before birth.

Luke 1:41, 44 also point to the humanness of the unborn child. John the Baptist is said to have "leaped" in Elizabeth's womb "for joy" when Mary's greeting was heard. John's prenatal recognition of the presence of Mary, the mother of the divine Messiah, points to his spiritual and rational capacity in the unborn state. Appropriately, the term used to describe John in his prenatal state is *baby,* the Greek term used for a child before and after birth (cf. Luke 2:12, 16; 18:15; 2 Tim. 3:15). Psalm 51:5 and Luke 1:41, 44 reflect the scriptural view that unborn children are spiritual, rational, moral beings. A baby, then, is "in the image of God" in the unborn state. Frame remarks, "There is nothing in Scripture that even remotely suggests that the unborn child is anything less than a human person from the moment of conception."[32]

One other argument which lends support to the humanness of the unborn baby is the traducian view of the origin of the soul. According to the creation theory of the origin of the soul, each human being is created by God and joined to the body at conception, birth, or sometime between. The major objection to this view is that sin must be imputed to each soul after its creation, or else God is creating a sinful being. According to the traducian view, the soul as well as the material part of man is "transferred" by human generation. Thus the whole human race was potentially in Adam. This position is consistent with the scriptural view of the human race as a corporate unity (cf. Acts 17:26; Rom. 5:12). The human race was seminally present in Adam and participated in his original sin (Rom. 5:12; cf. Heb. 7:9-10). The point here is that the soul is present in the unborn child. Since there is moral accountability in the prenatal state, the unborn child must be fully human.

Some feminists have suggested that a distinction between abortion and contraception is inappropriate, for the goal of both is the prevention of an unwanted birth.[33] However, there is a considerable difference between contraception and abortion. Contraception prevents the fertilization of the ovum by the sperm, neither of which alone can generate human life. Abortion, on the other hand, destroys what has already been conceived. In abortion a third party is involved—a unique individual whom God has made. Abortion is an insult to the creative work of God and a transgression against the very image of God in man.

IS ABORTION EVER JUSTIFIABLE?

Is abortion justifiable in the case of rape, incest, or deformity of the unborn child? While these are volatile and emotionally charged issues, they do not focus on the major problem facing America. Abortions in the United States for rape, incest, protection of the mother's life, or voiding of a deformed fetus comprise less than five percent of all abortions.[34] The rest of the abortions being done today are performed mainly for convenience—for purposes of birth control. However, these other difficult issues must be considered.

Rape

Rape rarely results in pregnancy. A ten-year study in Minnesota showed that no pregnancies resulted from 3,500 cases of forcible rape.[35] Conception can be prevented if the rape victim will seek treatment at a hospital immediately.

But what if a pregnancy should occur? It is a strange sort of justice that allows an innocent child to be killed for the crime of its father. The baby would still be the mother's own flesh and blood, no matter who the father was. Aborting the baby does not end the trauma of the rape; it compounds the sin of the

215

father. One should consider this question: "If you found out today that you were the product of a rape, would you wish that your mother had aborted you?"

Incest

Just as in the case of rape, special counsel and care is essential for a pregnant victim of incest. But aborting the baby would further jeopardize the physical and emotional well-being of the victim. Abortions performed on young girls are unusually hazardous, and studies show that sterility is as high as 30 percent among women 15 to 17 years of age who have had abortions.[36] As with rape, the child conceived by incest is a family member and should be cared for as such.

Protection

In the abortion controversy, most people think that "protecting the life of the mother" has to do with her physical well-being. Legally, however, the "protection of the mother" may include psychological, social, and economic considerations as well. C. Everett Koop, former Surgeon General of the United States and a leading pediatric surgeon, has stated, "In my thirty-six years in pediatric surgery I have never known of one instance where the child had to be aborted to save the mother's life."[37] In the rare case where a pregnancy must be abbreviated to protect the life of the mother, the proper procedure would be to give the child extraordinary care with the hopes of bringing it to maturity.[38]

Deformity

By examining a sample of the amniotic fluid in the womb (a process called "amniocentesis"), it is possible for a physician to determine if some deformity or defect is in the unborn child. If this test indicates that the child is deformed, should the child be aborted? When Moses questioned his own ability to speak to Pharaoh, God said, "Who gave man his mouth? Who makes him deaf or dumb? Who gives him sight or makes him blind? Is it not I, the Lord?" (Ex. 4:11). A sovereign God has the rightful authority to make some children "imperfect." These children are special because, as with the man born blind (John 9:3), God can use these handicaps to His glory.

Christians must not minimize the gravity of rape, incest, possible deformity, or danger to the life of the mother due to pregnancy. These infrequent and rather unique situations must be handled with scriptural counsel and loving concern. But situationalism must not govern decision-making in the area of Christian ethics. God is the One who creates life in the womb, and only He has the right to take it (Deut. 32:39; 1 Sam. 2:6).

WHAT CAN CHRISTIANS DO ABOUT ABORTION?

Christians have a moral and ethical responsibility to do something about abortion (cf. Prov. 24:11-14). Like the prophets of old, evangelical believers must cry out against the social and moral injustices so prevalent today (cf. Isa. 10:1-2; Jer. 2:34-35; Ezek. 22:3; Micah 3:9-10). Specifically, what can and should believers do about abortion?

Information

One of the biggest problems in the abortion issue is that most people do not know the facts about abortion. Thus, the first thing that believers should do is become more informed on this important issue. Literature on abortion from a Christian perspective is available from groups like the Christian Action Council. Most informed Christians will make a decision to be morally opposed to abortion.

Prayer

Concerned Christians are praying that Congress will pass a

"Human Life Bill." Many believers are praying for a Human Life Amendment to the Constitution so that unborn children can receive the same protection as other Americans. Prayer can influence state and national leaders to take a pro-life stand on the abortion issue.

Support

Christians should know the positions of their political candidates regarding abortion, and should support those who share their convictions regarding the value of unborn human life. At the same time, they should not support candidates who favor abortions nor institutions that provide abortion services (e.g., health plans, charity funds, hospitals).

Counsel

In counseling someone with an untimely pregnancy, one may help save the life of an unborn baby. Many pregnant mothers need counseling, housing, and help in finding adoptive parents for their babies.

Compassion

The more one learns about abortion, the more he may become angry. But he must be compassionate in dealing with those who have had abortions. Christians should hate the sin, but share Christ's love for the sinner (cf. Rom. 5:8). Many women who have abortions are the victims of exploitation. They are exploited first by men who want sex without responsibility, and then by physicians who are primarily interested in profiting from the lucrative abortion industry. Often those who have had abortions later become the most actively involved advocates for the unborn.

NOTES

1. Merrill McLoughlin, "America's New Civil War," *U.S. News and World Report*, 3 October 1988, 24.

2. Bill Horlacher, "Abortion: What Does the Bible Say?" *Worldwide Challenge*, July 1978, 6.

3 Susan T. Foh, "Abortion and Women's Lib," in *Thou Shalt Not Kill*, ed. Richard L. Ganz (New Rochelle, N.Y.: Arlington House Publishers, 1978), 51.

4. *New Practical Standard Dictionary*, ed. Charles Earle Funk, 1964 ed., s.v. "Abortion," 5.

5. John Lippis, *The Challenge to Be "Pro Life"* (Santa Barbara, Calif.: Santa Barbara Pro Life Education, 1978), 5–7; C. Everett Koop, "A Physician Looks at Abortion," in *Thou Shalt Not Kill*, 10–12.

6. J.C. Willke, *Abortion: How It Is* (Cincinnati: Hayes Publishing Co., 1972), 6–7.

7. John Willke, *Handbook on Abortion* (Cincinnati: Hayes Publishing Co., 1975), 83. One reason for the great range in figures reported is that the majority of abortion-caused deaths do not occur during the procedure, but only afterward due to complications.

8. Lippis, *The Challenge to Be "Pro Life,"* 7.

9. Ibid., 8. See also C. Everett Koop, "A Physician Looks at Abortion," 12–18, for a full disclosure.

10. Harold O.J. Brown, *Death before Life* (Nashville: Thomas Nelson Publishers, 1977), 74.

11. Ibid., 83–84.

12. Meredith G. Kline, "Lex Talionis and the Human Fetus," *Journal of the Evangelical Theological Society* 20 (September 1977): 193.

13. Ibid., 200–201.

14. Cf. Bruce K. Waltke, "Old Testament Texts Bearing on Abortion," *Christianity Today*, 8 November 1968, 99–105; and Bruce K. Waltke, "Old Testament Texts Bearing on the Issues" in *Birth Control and the Christian*, ed. W.O. Spitzer and Carlyle L. Saylor (Wheaton, Ill.: Tyndale House Publishers, 1969): 10–11. Waltke has since conceded that the support for this position is less than conclusive.

15. Bernard S. Jackson, "The Problem of Exod. XXI:22.5 (Lex Talionis)," *Vetus Testamentum* 23 (1973), 292.

16. C.F. Keil and F. Delitzsch, "Exodus," in vol. 2: *The Pentateuch*, 3 vols., trans. James Martin, *Commentary on the Old Testament* (reprint ed., Grand Rapids: Wm. B. Eerdmans Publishing Co., 1949), 134–35.

17. Jack W. Cottrell, "Abortion and the Mosaic Law," *Christianity Today,* 16 March 1973, 8.

18. Umberto Cassuto, *Commentary on the Book of Exodus,* trans. Israel Abrahams (Jerusalem: Magnes Press, 1967), 275.

19. John M. Frame, "Abortion from a Biblical Perspective," in *Thou Shalt Not Kill,* 56.

20. Brown, *Death before Life,* 126.

21. *Theological Word Book of the Old Testament,* ed. R. Laird Harris, Gleason L. Archer, and Bruce K. Waltke, 2 vols., s.v. by T. E. McComiskey, 1:396.

22. Ronald Barclay Allen, *In Celebrating Love of Life* (Portland, Ore.: Western Conservative Baptist Seminary, 1977), 6.

23. This translation of verse 13 is provided by Allen, *Love of Life.* His accurate and forceful translation of Psalm 139 is used throughout this consideration of the psalm.

24. A. Cohen suggests that this is possibly an allusion to the veins and arteries which are woven through the body like colored threads *(The Psalms,* Soncino Books of the Bible [London: Soncino Press, 1945], 453).

25. Francis Brown, S.R. Driver, and Charles A. Briggs, *A Hebrew and English Lexicon of the Old Testament* (Oxford: At the Clarendon Press, 1967), s.v. "slg," 166.

26. *The American Heritage Dictionary of the English Language,* ed. William Morris, 1969 ed., s.v. "embryo," 426.

27. Charles C. Ryrie, *You Mean the Bible Teaches That?* (Chicago: Moody Press, 1974), 89.

28. For a well-illustrated presentation of the week-by-week development of the womb, see *A Child Is Born: The Drama of Life before Birth,* by Axel Ingelman-Sundberg (New York: Dell Publishing Co., 1966), 11–156.

29. See Bruce K. Waltke, "Reflections from the Old Testament on Abortion," *Journal of the Evangelical Theological Society* 19 (Winter 1976): 10–13.

30. *Baker's Dictionary of Theology,* ed. Everett F. Harrison, 1960 ed., s.v. "Man," by Carl F.H. Henry, 340.

31. H.C. Leupold, *Exposition of the Psalms* (Grand Rapids: Baker Book House, 1959): 403.

32. Frame, "Abortion from a Biblical Perspective," 50–51.

33. Lucina Cisler, "Unfinished Business: Birth Control and Women's Liberation" in *Sisterhood Is Powerful,* ed. Robin Morgan (New York: Vintage Books, 1970), 299.

34. C. Everett Koop, "Deception-on-Demand," *Moody Monthly,* May 1980, 24.

35. Lippis, *The Challenge to Be "Pro Life,"* 9.
36. Koop, "Deception-on-Demand," 24.
37. Ibid., 26.
38. Ectopic pregnancy refers to the implantation of the fertilized ovum somewhere outside the uterus. Tubal pregnancy is the most frequent of all ectopic pregnancies. This condition is usually detected by hemorrhaging and requires immediate medical attention. Major abdominal surgery is mandatory to remove the embryo before it ruptures the fallopian tube; neglecting treatment will allow the tube to burst, resulting in uncontrollable hemorrhaging and usually the death of the mother. This surgery is not considered "abortion" for its purpose is to prevent the death of the mother, not prevent the birth of the child. Perhaps with medical advances, physicians will eventually be able to relocate and preserve the living embryo (cf. Brown, *Death before Life,* 22–23).

16
A BIBLICAL APPRAISAL OF THE AIDS EPIDEMIC
J. Kerby Anderson

A IDS, though first noted in the late 1970s, was not formally defined until 1982. Yet in less than a decade it has gone from near obscurity to front-page headlines and threats on large segments of the world's population.

The spread of the disease through the U.S. population has been staggering. In the early 1980s, about 200 Americans had been diagnosed with the virus. By the end of the 1980s, 50,000 had died from the disease, and the problem will grow worse in the 1990s.

BASIC INFORMATION ABOUT AIDS

What is AIDS?

AIDS is an acronym which stands for acquired immune deficiency syndrome. The AIDS virus is known as the human immunodeficiency virus (HIV). The virus can destroy a body's immune system so that it cannot fight off infections. Eventually a person with the HIV virus succumbs to life-threatening infections and opportunistic diseases including unusual forms of pneumonia and cancer.

The origin of AIDS is uncertain, although many trace its origins to central Africa. The green monkey of Africa carries a virus similar to AIDS, and many researchers believe that the virus was transmitted by monkeys to people.[1] Apparently those infected with the virus either moved to other countries or infected American tourists, who brought the disease to this country.

Although AIDS seems to have come to the United States much earlier than the 1970s, it was only formally identified in 1982 when doctors had been working to identify a previously unknown disease. Within five years after its formal identification, AIDS had already spread rapidly. By September 1987, there were 41,825 Americans diagnosed as having AIDS. Of those AIDS victims, only 17,755 were still alive.[2]

While getting accurate numbers for the number diagnosed with the disease may be difficult, getting an accurate estimate for the number infected with the HIV virus is even more difficult. In 1987, the Centers for Disease Control (CDC) estimated that 900,000 to 1.4 million Americans were infected with the HIV virus. Although CDC believed the actual number of persons with the virus was much higher due to underreporting, they believed that the actual number of people with the HIV virus would be only about 10 percent higher.[3] By contrast, the Hudson Institute, using a mathematical model, placed their estimate more than twice as high as the CDC. The Hudson Institute report said that its "best guess at the range of total infections as of year-end 1987 was from 1.9 million to 3 million persons, with the likeliest range between 2.2 million and 2.6 million people."[4]

Stages of AIDS

Physicians have identified three stages of the progression of AIDS. Stage one is the asymptomatic carrier stage. The individual in this stage is infected with the HIV virus but shows no discernible signs or symptoms of AIDS. Unless people have had a blood test, they may be unaware they have the disease. Nevertheless, a person in this stage can infect others with the virus even though they do not manifest any visible sign of infection. A person may remain in this stage for a number of years.

The second stage is AIDS-Related Complex (ARC). This stage progresses from the first when an individual begins to show some of the symptoms of HIV infection. Such symptoms include sudden unexplained weight loss, night sweating, diarrhea, swelling of the lymph nodes, neurologic disorders (memory loss, partial paralysis, or loss of coordination), and chronic fatigue.

The third stage is full-blown AIDS. This stage is characterized by opportunistic infections which occur due to a deficiency of the person's immune system. A healthy immune system would normally protect against the damaging effects of these diseases, but the HIV impairs the normal immune protection system and these infections continue to weaken and eventually kill the person infected with the HIV virus.

Diseases of AIDS

When AIDS is in the final stage, it is frequently diagnosed on the basis of one or more of the following opportunistic diseases:

1. Kaposi sarcoma—an invasive form of skin cancer which also affects the internal organs (lungs, lumph nodes, liver, stomach, intestines).
2. Pneumocystis carinii—a form of pneumonia, a parasitic infection that affects the lungs and can ultimately lead to suffocation.
3. Candidiasis—a fungal infection which produces white patches in the mouth and makes it difficult to swallow.
4. Cytomegalovirus—a viral infection which affects the lungs and can spread throughout the body.
5. Herpes simplex—an infection that often produces severe ulcers around the mouth and perianal areas.
6. Herpes zoster—oozing blisters and large black scabs over oral, nasal, and rectal areas.
7. Toxoplasmosis—an intracellular parasite often found in cat

feces which produces such symptoms as headaches, fever, and vomiting.

8. Cryptosporidiosis—a fungal infection which can cause meningitis. Symptoms can include mental disturbances and personality changes.

Transmission of AIDS

The HIV virus is transmitted through the exchange of infected bodily fluids. Some 89 percent of persons known to have AIDS are homosexuals or intravenous drug abusers. Another 3 percent became infected through blood transfusions (most before blood banks began testing for the AIDS antibody), 1 percent are infants and children, and 3 percent are undetermined.[5]

This leaves 4 percent of known AIDS patients who became infected with the disease through heterosexual contact. Some health officials estimate that in the 1990s the number of AIDS cases acquired through heterosexual contact will increase to 6 percent of all cases, though this is still a matter of some debate in the medical community.[6]

A more alarming statistic is that based upon the 1986 Surgeon General's Report: We have at least 1.5 million carriers of the HIV virus in the United States.[7] Most of these people do not know they are carriers and thus may be unknowingly spreading the virus through sexual activity or intravenous drug use.

Although there is some disagreement about the number of modes in which the AIDS virus can be transmitted, there is near universal agreement that it can be transmitted in at least four major ways.

1. Sexual activity—the HIV can be spread through the contact of infected sexual discharges with mucous membranes. This occurs most frequently through anal or vaginal sex, but has also been documented for oral sex as well.

2. IV drug use—sharing drug needles and syringes with an infected person can spread the virus.

3. Transfusion—infected blood or blood products can transmit

the HIV virus as well, especially to hemophiliacs who require frequent blood transfusions.

4. Perinatal—an AIDS-infected mother can pass the virus to her child during pregnancy, labor, or delivery.

The primary mode in which the HIV virus is spread is through blood, semen, or vaginal secretions. The virus has also been found in other body fluids such as saliva, tears, breast milk, and urine. Yet there is scant evidence that AIDS is passed through casual contact. The Public Health Service has stated that there is no evidence to suggest a risk of contracting the HIV virus from day-to-day social or family contact with someone who has AIDS.[8]

An AIDS study reported in the *New England Journal of Medicine* in 1987 supported this conclusion. Doctors studied the nonsexual household contacts of patients with AIDS or ARC (AIDS-related complex). The study analyzed 101 household contacts (68 children and 33 adults) who had contact with one of the 39 AIDS patients for at least a three-month period. There was a sharing of household items (razors, combs, towels, clothes, drinking glasses), of household facilities (bed, toilet, bath, kitchen), and of washing items used by the patients (dishes, bath). Moreover, there was a measurable amount of social interaction (shaking hands, hugging, kissing). Yet the doctors found only 1 out of the 101 household contacts had evidence of infection with the virus. This was a five-year-old who most likely acquired the virus perinatally.[9]

This, however, does not mean that the AIDS virus can never be spread in what might be deemed "casual contact." Dr. Jerome Groopman of Harvard and Dr. Robert Gallo of the National Cancer Institute reported in the British medical journal *Lancet* that saliva was the mode of transmission from a man with transfusion-acquired AIDS to his wife. And in the same journal, two years later, one documented case of non-sexual within-family transmission of AIDS was reported.[10]

Also, the Centers for Disease Control released a report in 1987 that stated that three hospital workers tested positive for the HIV virus after their skin came into contact with the blood of AIDS patients. One was infected when a vacuum-sealed test tube popped open and splashed blood into her mouth. Another was an emergency room nurse who applied pressure where a catheter had been removed from an artery. And the third had been splattered with blood from a lab machine.[11]

Finally, an epidemiological study at several laboratories working with the HIV virus identified one worker who became infected. The individual infected worked at a facility where high concentrated quantities of HIV were being produced, and may not have been wearing all of the standard protective garments.[12]

AIDS POLICY

AIDS Education

The foundation of a comprehensive AIDS policy is education. This has been seen by many activists as the primary means of fighting the AIDS epidemic.

Certainly education is an important weapon. Many in our society are ignorant of the facts and need more information. For example, a study of young people in San Francisco revealed that 30 percent believed AIDS could be cured if treated early, and one-third did not know that AIDS cannot be transmitted by merely touching someone with AIDS.[13]

So providing the facts about AIDS is important. But often this is done in a so-called "value neutral" environment. Educators and counselors attempt to discuss AIDS and human sexuality in an amoral framework. But in attempting to be amoral, they often end up being immoral. Teaching the facts about subjects like condoms and homosexuality without teaching the moral values associated with them is tantamount to encouraging immorality.

Moreover, there is some question about the general effectiveness of AIDS education. While educating students about AIDS may help provide them with the basic facts about AIDS, we should not be so naive as to believe that it will necessarily change behavior. Human sin nature (Rom. 3:23) frequently keeps us from doing what is right and leads us to practice evil (Rom. 7:15-19).

This was evident in a survey of students at the University of Maryland about their knowledge of AIDS and their subsequent sexual behavior. Seventy-seven percent said they knew condoms can be used to limit the risk of infection of AIDS, but only 30 percent reported increased use of condoms. Eighty-three percent of the male students who said they have homosexual relations said they had made no change in their behavior.[14]

Finally, AIDS education sometimes misrepresents the facts. Various medical and governmental reports have touted the condom as an effective means of reducing the risk of contracting AIDS. While it may be true that condoms reduce the risk, they by no means eliminate the risk. When condoms are used for contraceptive purposes, they fail about 10 percent of the time over the course of a year. Former Surgeon General C. Everett Koop warned of the "extraordinarily high" failure rate of condoms among homosexuals. And a study done at the University of Miami Medical School showed that 17 percent of the women whose husbands with AIDS used condoms became infected themselves within a year despite the use of condoms.[15]

AIDS Testing

AIDS testing is one of the more controversial aspects of developing a comprehensive AIDS policy. The Reagan Administration had proposed routine testing at all clinics and hospitals[16] although there was some debate within the administration about mandatory testing.[17] The American Medical Association rejected the idea of mandatory testing but instead adopted a draft report recommending routine testing at clinics that treat sexually transmitted diseases and drug abuse.[18] Both called for mandatory AIDS testing for immigrants and prison inmates.[19]

Although testing for AIDS has generally been endorsed as wise AIDS policy, there are still many who argue that education is the only weapon against AIDS and therefore reject attempts to expand AIDS testing. While education about AIDS is necessary and helpful, education alone is not the answer. If AIDS education were the sole answer, then the numerous VD education programs would have substantially reduced the number of sexually transmitted diseases cases.

Advocates of an "education-only" policy ignore the educational value of testing. Public health officials estimate that only a small percentage of people who carry the HIV virus know they have it. Routine AIDS testing would inform them of that fact and allow them to receive additional information and counseling from health care workers.

Those who test positively for the IIIV virus must be told to adjust their behavior. If they don't have the test, they most likely will be unaware of their condition and probably will not adjust their behavior.

Everyone uses selective perception to screen out most of the messages they receive. We don't, for example, pay much attention to a lawnmower commercial unless we are in the market for a lawnmower. So if people don't think they are at risk for AIDS, the educational information may not get through a person's perceptual screen.

In addition to selective perception is the problem of emotional denial. High-risk groups often ignore messages they don't want to hear. AIDS testing will alert carriers of their need for more information about AIDS and provide a context for individual education and counseling with those carrying the virus.

Finally, Scripture clearly teaches that those who often engage in practices that spread AIDS will "suppress the truth in unrighteousness" (Rom. 1:18). So AIDS testing must be used to alert those carrying the HIV virus to the nature of their condition.

Critics of AIDS testing say it is costly and unreliable. Both concerns are unwarranted. A single test is very inexpensive and certainly a worthy investment in order to alert those who unknowingly are carrying the AIDS virus.

The AIDS test is also very reliable, especially when multiple testing is used. Blood reacting positive to an ELISA (enzyme-linked immunosorbent assay) test is tested two more times. If one or both of those tests are positive, the blood is then subjected to the Western Blot test. If that blood tests positive, another blood sample is taken and a second Western Blot test administered to confirm the previous results. According to Dr. Fred Darr, medical director of American Red Cross Blood Services, "When a person is Western blot confirmed, that has a very, very, very high degree of reliablity. It's like finger-printing the [AIDS] antibody, and it's very, very specific. Reli-ability of the Western blot test is very high."[20]

AIDS testing should not be seen as an impediment to educa-tion but rather an aid to education. Testing educates the indi-vidual by alerting him or her to the presence of the AIDS virus. Such information can prevent the further transmission of the disease. Testing educates society by providing important epidemiological information about the development and spread of this disease.

AIDS Quarantine

An even more controversial aspect of AIDS policy is quaran-tine. Unlike many infectious diseases, AIDS cannot be spread through casual, non-sexual contact. So a universal quarantine woud be useless and unwarranted. However, limited quaran-tine or isolation may be warranted when a person with the HIV virus persists in engaging in dangerous behavior that risks spreading the virus to others.

Critics of quarantine argue it is too harsh and shows a lack of concern for the tragic victims of this disease. But concern for AIDS victims should not obscure our critical need to make difficult, and seemingly harsh, public health decisions in order to protect the rest of society.

Unfortunately, efforts to control AIDS have been clouded by

talk of civil liberties violations which have hampered public health officials' abilities to act in the public interest. One of the most vicious confrontations to date was waged over the brief closure of gay bathhouses in San Francisco and New York. Although the Centers for Disease Control eventually endorsed state and local efforts to regulate or close these bathhouses,[21] many remain open.

Opponents of these actions argue that public health officials should focus their sole attention on a massive education program which promotes methods of having "safe sex." But a faulty assumption in the "safe sex" campaign is the presupposition that AIDS carriers will be concerned about transmitting the virus and want to restrict their activities.

A number of AIDS victims are too sexually promiscuous to be concerned with the consequences of their actions. Health care workers at an Alameda, California, clinic frequently treated one homosexual man with AIDS who has admitted to having sexual relations with three to five different men each week without telling them of his condition. Dr. Robert Benjamin of the Alameda County Bureau of Communicable Diseases laments he is unable to do anything about this man since he hasn't broken any laws.[22]

Other victims spread the disease out of vengeance. Brazilian psychiatrist Ana Maria de Souza Barbosa reports that one of her patients who is dying of AIDS vowed to have sexual relations with as many partners as possible during Brazil's annual Carnival celebration.[23]

Still other victims spread the disease out of financial necessity. New York physician Mark Kaplan has a prostitute with AIDS for a patient who he wishes he could "keep off the streets."[24]

In these particular situations, quarantine may be an effective tool in preventing the spread of the disease. When AIDS victims willfully persist in spreading this disease, government must intervene.

One mode of quarantine would be a form of house arrest. A prostitute in Florida who has AIDS wore an electronic monitoring device to ensure her compliance with a house-arrest so that she did not spread the disease.[25]

In other circumstances, a true quarantine might have to be considered. Dr. Vernon Mark of Harvard Medical School recommended that the state declare AIDS a "dangerous transmissible disease" so that the state could take extraordinary measures. Carriers of the disease would be notified that if they continued being sexually promiscuous or sharing needles, they would be quarantined on Penikese Island (a former leper colony off the coast of Cape Cod).[26]

AIDS AND THE BIBLE

Although the Bible does not say anything specifically about AIDS, it does address the issues of sexual promiscuity and homosexuality. When the Apostle Paul warned that "he who sins sexually sins against his own body" (1 Cor. 6:18), he was not warning against AIDS. But there are physical consequences (such as sexually transmitted diseases) to sexual promiscuity.

When Paul, talking about homosexuality, said they "received in themselves the due penalty for their perversion" (Rom. 1:27), he was most likely talking about a spiritual penalty. Nevertheless, there are physical penalties to homosexual relations as well.

AIDS and Homosexuality

Gay activists constantly state that AIDS is "not just a gay disease," and that is true. But it is a disease that has struck a disproportionately large number of homosexuals and has been spread through its sexual mode of transmission through homosexual and bisexual sex.

We cannot ignore the homosexual factor, but neither should we overemphasize it. In Africa, for example, AIDS is a heterosexual disease which affects men and women equally. There-

232

fore, they perceive it more as a venereal disease rather than a homosexual disease.[27]

Christians must respond to AIDS and homosexuality with both biblical convictions and biblical compassion. First, we must respond with biblical convictions about what the Bible says about homosexuality.

The Bible clearly teaches that homosexuality is an abomination to God (Lev. 18:22). It is not an alternative lifestyle. In fact, Scripture teaches that it is unnatural (Rom. 1:26-27).

The Bible also teaches that God will judge homosexuality (Gen. 19:1-26; Jud. 19:1-30; Lev. 20:13; Rom. 1:18-27; 1 Cor. 6:9-10; 1 Tim. 1:8-11).

Second, we must respond with biblical compassion to those suffering with AIDS. Christ came into the world to save sinners (1 Tim. 1:15), including those caught up in the sin of homosexuality. Christ died for homosexuals and can by His grace deliver them from their practices (1 Cor. 6:11). They can become new creatures (2 Cor. 5:17) and break the bondage of sin in their lives.

Is AIDS a Judgment of God?

Because AIDS has often been considered a "gay plague," the homosexual community has accused the government of apathy and indifference. These charges were frequently followed by recriminations from certain Christian leaders that AIDS was a judgment from God on homosexuals.

But if AIDS is indeed God's hand of judgment on homosexuals, it is certainly an indiscriminate one. AIDS strikes seemingly innocent children through blood transfusions and leaves lesbians intact (one of the lowest-risk categories for contracting the disease).

If AIDS is a judgment from God, it is a judgment in the sense that all disease is the result of God's judgment on this earth because of the Fall (Gen. 3). Sometime God may directly judge sinful disobedience by striking a person with a disease. Cotton Mather taught, for example, that "Sickness is in fact the whip of God for the sins of many." But more often, diseases like AIDS are the logical consequence of disobedience to God's word.

AIDS, like a host of other sexually transmitted diseases (STDs), is the logical consequence of sinful behavior. All of these STDs (herpes, chlamydia, syphilis, gonorrhea) are the natural consequences of sexual disobedience. In the case of AIDS, homosexual promiscuity was the triggering mechanism. Homosexual sex was the sowing that led to the reaping of AIDS.

Unfortunately, so many others have been and will be victims of this wanton promiscuity and eventually contract the disease and die. In a sense, this is the payment a society pays for tolerating, and even in some cases encouraging, an immoral lifestyle.

We have a responsibility to both condemn the sin and cure the sinner. Christians frequently seem caught in the false dilemma of Albert Camus' novel *The Plague*. Should Christians help man (and fight the plague) or obey God (and let the plague continue)? In our current context some seem to be asking: Should Christians try to cure AIDS, or would that be going against the will of God?

Camus develops a false disjunctive in his novel which Christians have often unconsciously accepted. The priest believes that the plague must be endured but not resisted. The doctor can't accept the priests' belief that everything (including the plague) is decreed according to God's sovereign perfecting.

This is a false dichotomy. When Christians use medicine to cure disease (even sexually transmitted disease), they are fulfilling the dominion covenant (Gen. 1:28), not crossing the Lord's will. When they work to alleviate suffering, they are working to alleviate the "wrath of God" poured out on the earth as a result of the Fall (Gen. 3; Rom. 8:20-25).

Christians don't have to choose between helping man and serving God. They should be preaching against unrighteousness and calling for homosexuals to repent of their immoral lifestyles. At the same time, they should be ministering to

AIDS victims and calling for further medical research to find a cure for AIDS. The two positions are not contradictory but complementary commands of Scripture.

MINISTRY IN THE AIDS EPIDEMIC

Churches and individual Christians can and should have a ministry to AIDS victims in their communities. An important first step is preparing the pastor and church staff for AIDS ministry.

Pastoral Preparation

Pastors and their church staffs must prepare themselves in advance for many of the challenges of ministering to those afflicted with AIDS. The first step is education. Pastors and their staff must understand the nature of AIDS and HIV infection. Understanding the modes of HIV transmission will alleviate many unwarranted fears and can be helpful in developing a church AIDS policy. Pastors must stay current on research developments, health resources, and legal issues concerning AIDS.

A second step is mental preparation. Pastors and their staffs must resolve their fear of AIDS. First, there is the personal fear of possibly contracting the disease through casual contact. Although there should be little concern about this, our emotions may cause us to act differently. Recently, when a group of elders visited a family in their church whose baby was dying of AIDS, they refrained from laying hands on the baby when they prayed (James 5:14-15). There is also the fear that associating with AIDS victims would be misunderstood as condoning a lifestyle. Since a large percentage of AIDS victims are homosexuals or drug users, pastors might fear that their ministry to these victims could be perceived as accepting these lifestyles.

A third step in preparation is to locate resources and organizations that can help. Government agencies as well as local agencies exist to help provide care and resources for AIDS victims. Also, support groups and even ministry groups often exist and should be identified in the local community to augment the ministry at the local church.

Pastoral Counseling

AIDS, like many other diseases, provides a number of opportunities for counseling and other forms of ministry. A primary opportunity for counseling will be with the AIDS patient. This should take place in three areas.

First, pastors and other counselors should provide education. The AIDS patient must have a comprehensive understanding of the disease. This would include a functional understanding of the health care needs and a warning of the danger of transmitting the virus to others.

Second, pastors and counselors should provide emotional and spiritual encouragement. They should affirm the patient's self-worth through consistent contact (including physical contact). Pastors may also deal with the issue of a sinful lifestyle and direct the patient toward confession and repentance (1 John 1:9). And the counselor can facilitate the need for reconciliation: first to God through confession or profession, and second to parents and family through communication.

Third, pastors and counselors should strive to meet the practical needs of an AIDS patient. They can help secure financial assistance for health care needs. They can anticipate daily needs (groceries, laundry, housecleaning). And they can provide counseling and direction in a time of grief and preparation for death.

Another opportunity for ministry and counseling would be with the family (parents, spouse, children) of the AIDS patient. Pastors and counselor can help identify and resolve the fears. They can facilitate reconciliation and communication among the family. And they can facilitate the grief process and provide preparation for death.

A BIBLICAL APPRAISAL OF THE AIDS EPIDEMIC

Church Policy

As the number of AIDS cases in society increases, the pressure on churches to act will increase. This disease provides an opportunity to preach against the folly of the world's unrighteousness and to teach the wisdom of biblical principles of human sexuality. But, as has just been delineated, the church can and should do much more than just preach on this subject.

An effective tool in organizing and coordinating an individual church's response to the AIDS epidemic is to establish a written church policy. Many evangelical churches have already done this so that church staff, elders, teachers, and nursery workers know what their legal, moral, and biblical responsibilities should be.[28]

Communicating this policy to the congregation will help educate the congregation and dispel some of the fear and prejudice that result from a lack of information on the subject of AIDS. It will also provide procedures for members of the congregation to follow and protect the congregation from the real dangers of HIV transmission.

An adequate church policy must both protect the uninfected and provide care for the ill. Christians must exercise wisdom in order to prevent contagion, but also must exercise compassion in order to meet the physical, emotional, and spiritual needs of AIDS victims.

NOTES

1. Robert Redfield and Wanda Kay Franz, *AIDS and Young People* (Washington, D.C.: Regnery Gateway, 1987), 5.

2. *AIDS and the Education of Our Children* (Washington, D.C.: U.S. Department of Education, 1987), 1.

3. Ibid.

4. "Government AIDS estimate too low, study finds," *New Dimensions,* Special issue, 1989, 8.

5. "Mode of transmission for persons with AIDS," *AIDS Weekly Surveillance Report* (Atlanta: Centers for Disease Control, 14 September 1987).

6. *AIDS and the Education of Our Children,* 3.

7. C. Everett Koop, *The Surgeon General's Report on Acquired Immune Deficiency Syndrome* (Washington: U.S. Department of Health and Human Services, 1986), 12.

8. *AIDS and the Education of Our Children,* 4.

9. Gerald Friedland, Brian Saltzman, and Martha Rogers, "Lack of transmission of HTLV-III/LAV infection to household contacts of patients with AIDS or AIDS related complex with oral candidiasis," *The New England Journal of Medicine* (6 February 1987): 344–349.

10. Jerome Groopman and Robert Gallo, *The Lancet,* December 22/29, 1984 and *The Lancet,* September 20, 1986 both reported in article by Wayne Lutton, "Hazardous to your health," *National Review,* 30 January 1987, 54–55.

11. Jean Seligmann, "A new worry for health-care workers," *Newsweek,* 1 June 1987, 55.

12. Joseph Palcs, "Lab worker infected with AIDS virus," *Nature,* 10 September 1987, 92.

13. *AIDS and the Education of Our Children,* 7.

14. Ibid, 7.

15. "Condoms and AIDS," *AIDS and the Education of Our Children,* 16.

16. Richard Stengel, "Testing Dilemma," *Time,* 8 June 1987, 20–22.

17. Terrence Monmaney, "AIDS: Who should be tested?" *Newsweek,* 11 May 1987, 64–65.

18. "AMA backs more testing for AIDS," *Dallas Times Herald,* 24 June 1987, A-1, 14.

19. "Mandatory AIDS tests for aliens, inmates backed by doctor's group," *Dallas Morning News,* 21 June 1987.

20. "Mandatory AIDS testing becomes hot political item," *Human Events,* 6 June 1987, 7.

21. "U.S. agency backs closing bathhouses," *Dallas Times Herald,* 8 November 1985.

22. Jerry Adler, "The AIDS conflict," *Newsweek,* 23 September 1985, 19.

23. "Brazil's easy sex, toleration falls victim to AIDS panic," *Dallas Times Herald,* 2 November 1985, 46.

24. Marilyn Chase, "Doctor's efforts to control AIDS spark battles over civil liberties," *Wall Street Journal,* 8 February 1985.

25. "Beeper to keep tabs on prostitute who has AIDS," *Dallas Times Herald,* 28 September 1985, 4A.

26. "Quarantine for AIDS?" *Newsweek,* 25 November 1985, 6.

27. A more detailed discussion of AIDS and homosexuality can be found in the article by Bill Lawrence, "No immunity," *Kindred Spirit,*

Autumn 1988, 12–14.
28. One model churches might want to emulate is the "Communicable Disease Policy" developed at Northwest Bible Church in Dallas, Texas in 1988.